50 Sourdough Bread Baking Recipes for Home

By: Kelly Johnson

Table of Contents

- Classic Sourdough Boule
- Whole Wheat Sourdough Bread
- Rye Sourdough Loaf
- Sourdough Baguettes
- Sourdough Ciabatta
- Sourdough Focaccia
- Sourdough Sandwich Bread
- Sourdough Dinner Rolls
- Sourdough English Muffins
- Sourdough Cinnamon Raisin Bread
- Sourdough Walnut Bread
- Sourdough Olive Bread
- Sourdough Jalapeno Cheddar Bread
- Sourdough Pumpernickel Bread
- Sourdough Challah
- Sourdough Brioche
- Sourdough Pretzels
- Sourdough Bagels
- Sourdough Pizza Crust
- Sourdough Flatbread
- Sourdough Crackers
- Sourdough Pancakes
- Sourdough Waffles
- Sourdough French Toast
- Sourdough Donuts
- Sourdough Banana Bread
- Sourdough Zucchini Bread
- Sourdough Pumpkin Bread
- Sourdough Chocolate Chip Bread
- Sourdough Apple Cinnamon Bread
- Sourdough Lemon Poppyseed Bread
- Sourdough Cranberry Orange Bread
- Sourdough Artisan Loaf with Herbs
- Sourdough Seeded Bread
- Sourdough Multigrain Bread

- Sourdough Spelt Bread
- Sourdough Kamut Bread
- Sourdough Einkorn Bread
- Sourdough Emmer Bread
- Sourdough Feta and Spinach Bread
- Sourdough Sun-Dried Tomato Bread
- Sourdough Asiago and Rosemary Bread
- Sourdough Pesto Swirl Bread
- Sourdough Olive Oil Bread
- Sourdough Honey Wheat Bread
- Sourdough Irish Soda Bread
- Sourdough Caramelized Onion Bread
- Sourdough Garlic Bread
- Sourdough Herb and Cheese Bread
- Sourdough Everything Bagel Bread

Classic Sourdough Boule

Ingredients:

- 1 cup active sourdough starter (100% hydration)
- 1 1/2 cups lukewarm water
- 4 cups bread flour
- 1 1/2 teaspoons salt

Instructions:

In a large mixing bowl, combine the active sourdough starter and lukewarm water. Stir until well combined.

Add the bread flour and salt to the bowl. Use a wooden spoon or your hands to mix until a shaggy dough forms.

Once the dough comes together, turn it out onto a lightly floured surface. Knead the dough for about 10-15 minutes, or until it becomes smooth and elastic.

Place the kneaded dough back into the mixing bowl. Cover the bowl with plastic wrap or a clean kitchen towel and let the dough rise at room temperature for about 4-6 hours, or until it has doubled in size. Alternatively, you can place the bowl in the refrigerator and let the dough rise overnight for enhanced flavor.

Once the dough has doubled in size, gently deflate it by pressing down on it with your fingertips.

Shape the dough into a round boule by pulling the edges towards the center and pinching them together. Flip the dough over so that the seam side is facing down.

Place the shaped boule onto a piece of parchment paper. Cover it loosely with plastic wrap or a kitchen towel and let it rise at room temperature for another 2-4 hours, or until it has puffed up slightly.

About 30 minutes before baking, preheat your oven to 450°F (230°C). Place a Dutch oven or heavy-bottomed pot with a lid into the oven to preheat as well.

Once the oven and pot are preheated, carefully remove the pot from the oven. Lift the parchment paper with the boule and carefully place it into the preheated pot. Cover the pot with the lid and bake the boule in the preheated oven for 20 minutes.

After 20 minutes, remove the lid from the pot and continue baking the boule for an additional 20-25 minutes, or until the crust is deep golden brown and the bread sounds hollow when tapped on the bottom.

Once done, remove the pot from the oven and transfer the boule to a wire rack to cool completely before slicing.

Enjoy your classic sourdough boule with your favorite spreads or as part of a meal!

This classic sourdough boule is perfect for slicing and enjoying with soups, sandwiches, or simply with butter and jam. The tangy flavor and chewy texture make it a favorite among sourdough enthusiasts.

Whole Wheat Sourdough Bread

Ingredients:

- 1 cup active sourdough starter
- 1 1/2 cups lukewarm water
- 4 cups bread flour
- 1 1/2 teaspoons salt

Instructions:

In a large mixing bowl, combine the active sourdough starter and lukewarm water. Stir until well mixed.

Add the bread flour and salt to the bowl. Use a wooden spoon or dough whisk to mix until a shaggy dough forms.

Once the dough comes together, turn it out onto a lightly floured surface. Knead the dough for about 10-15 minutes until it becomes smooth and elastic.

Place the kneaded dough back into the mixing bowl, cover with a clean kitchen towel or plastic wrap, and let it rest at room temperature for about 4-6 hours, or until doubled in size.

Once the dough has doubled in size, gently punch it down to release any air bubbles. Shape it into a round boule by tucking the edges underneath to create tension on the surface.

Place the shaped boule onto a piece of parchment paper and transfer it to a proofing basket or a bowl lined with a clean kitchen towel, seam side down.

Cover the boule with a kitchen towel or plastic wrap and let it proof at room temperature for about 1-2 hours, or until it has slightly puffed up.

About 30 minutes before the proofing time is up, preheat your oven to 450°F (230°C) with a Dutch oven or baking stone inside.

Once the oven is preheated, carefully transfer the proofed boule along with the parchment paper into the preheated Dutch oven or onto the baking stone.

Score the top of the boule with a sharp knife or bread lame to allow for expansion during baking.

Cover the Dutch oven with its lid or use a large oven-safe bowl to cover the boule.

Bake the covered boule in the preheated oven for 20 minutes. Then, remove the lid or covering and continue baking for an additional 20-25 minutes, or until the boule is golden brown and sounds hollow when tapped on the bottom.

Once baked, remove the boule from the oven and let it cool on a wire rack for at least 30 minutes before slicing.

Enjoy your Classic Sourdough Boule with your favorite spreads or as a side to soups and salads!

Whole Wheat Sourdough Bread

Ingredients:

- 1 cup active sourdough starter
- 1 1/2 cups lukewarm water
- 2 cups whole wheat flour
- 1 1/2 cups bread flour
- 1 1/2 teaspoons salt

Instructions:

In a large mixing bowl, combine the active sourdough starter and lukewarm water. Stir until well mixed.
Add the whole wheat flour, bread flour, and salt to the bowl. Use a wooden spoon or dough whisk to mix until a shaggy dough forms.
Once the dough comes together, turn it out onto a lightly floured surface. Knead the dough for about 10-15 minutes until it becomes smooth and elastic.
Place the kneaded dough back into the mixing bowl, cover with a clean kitchen towel or plastic wrap, and let it rest at room temperature for about 4-6 hours, or until doubled in size.
Once the dough has doubled in size, gently punch it down to release any air bubbles. Shape it into a loaf by tucking the edges underneath to create tension on the surface.
Place the shaped loaf into a greased loaf pan, cover with a kitchen towel or plastic wrap, and let it proof at room temperature for about 1-2 hours, or until it has slightly puffed up.
About 30 minutes before the proofing time is up, preheat your oven to 450°F (230°C).
Once the oven is preheated, bake the proofed loaf in the preheated oven for 30-35 minutes, or until the loaf is golden brown and sounds hollow when tapped on the bottom.
Once baked, remove the loaf from the oven and let it cool in the pan for 5 minutes. Then, transfer it to a wire rack to cool completely before slicing.
Enjoy your Whole Wheat Sourdough Bread with your favorite toppings or use it for sandwiches and toast!

These recipes will yield delicious and flavorful sourdough bread that you can enjoy with various meals or as a standalone treat. Adjust the fermentation times according to your sourdough starter's activity and your desired level of sourness. Enjoy your homemade sourdough bread!

Rye Sourdough Loaf

Ingredients:

- 400g bread flour
- 100g whole wheat flour
- 350g active sourdough starter (100% hydration)
- 320g lukewarm water
- 10g salt

Instructions:

In a large mixing bowl, combine the bread flour, whole wheat flour, active sourdough starter, and lukewarm water. Mix until a shaggy dough forms.
Cover the bowl with plastic wrap or a kitchen towel and let it rest for 30 minutes (autolyse).
After the autolyse, add the salt to the dough and knead until the salt is fully incorporated.
Transfer the dough to a clean, lightly floured surface and knead for about 10-15 minutes until the dough is smooth and elastic.
Place the dough in a lightly oiled bowl, cover with plastic wrap, and let it rise at room temperature until doubled in size, about 4-6 hours.
Once doubled, gently deflate the dough and shape it into a boule (round loaf).
Place the shaped boule on a floured surface or in a proofing basket, seam side down.
Cover the boule loosely with plastic wrap or a kitchen towel and let it rise for another 2-3 hours, until it has visibly expanded.
Preheat your oven to 450°F (230°C) with a Dutch oven or baking stone inside.
Score the top of the boule with a sharp knife or razor blade.
Carefully transfer the boule to the preheated Dutch oven or baking stone. Cover with the lid and bake for 20 minutes.
Remove the lid and continue baking for another 20-25 minutes, or until the boule is golden brown and sounds hollow when tapped on the bottom.
Remove the boule from the oven and let it cool on a wire rack before slicing.

Whole Wheat Sourdough Bread

Ingredients:

- 400g whole wheat flour
- 100g bread flour
- 350g active sourdough starter (100% hydration)
- 320g lukewarm water
- 10g salt

Instructions:

Follow the same instructions as above for mixing, kneading, and shaping the dough.
Proceed with the same rise and proofing times as described for the Classic Sourdough Boule.
Preheat your oven and bake the whole wheat sourdough boule following the same instructions as for the Classic Sourdough Boule.

Rye Sourdough Loaf:

Ingredients:

- 300g rye flour
- 200g bread flour
- 350g active sourdough starter (100% hydration)
- 320g lukewarm water
- 10g salt

Instructions:

Follow the same instructions as above for mixing, kneading, and shaping the dough.
Proceed with the same rise and proofing times as described for the Classic Sourdough Boule.

Preheat your oven and bake the rye sourdough loaf following the same instructions as for the Classic Sourdough Boule.

These recipes should yield delicious sourdough bread with different flavors and textures. Enjoy baking!

Sourdough Baguettes

Ingredients:

- 350g bread flour
- 150g sourdough starter (100% hydration)
- 225g lukewarm water
- 8g salt

Instructions:

In a large mixing bowl, combine the sourdough starter and lukewarm water. Mix until the starter is fully dissolved in the water.

Add the bread flour and salt to the bowl. Mix with a wooden spoon or your hands until a shaggy dough forms.

Transfer the dough to a clean, lightly floured surface. Knead the dough for about 10-15 minutes until it becomes smooth and elastic.

Place the dough in a lightly oiled bowl, cover with plastic wrap or a kitchen towel, and let it rest at room temperature for about 4-6 hours, or until it has doubled in size. This step may take longer depending on the activity of your sourdough starter and the temperature of your kitchen.

Once doubled in size, gently deflate the dough and divide it into two equal portions.

Shape each portion of dough into a baguette shape. To do this, flatten each portion of dough into a rectangle, then fold the top third down and the bottom third up, like folding a letter. Roll the dough into a log shape, then taper the ends slightly to form a baguette.

Place the shaped baguettes on a lightly floured surface or a baguette pan, if you have one. Cover with a kitchen towel and let them rise for another 1-2 hours, or until they have visibly expanded.

Meanwhile, preheat your oven to 450°F (230°C) and place a baking stone or upside-down baking sheet in the oven to preheat.

Just before baking, use a sharp knife or razor blade to make diagonal slashes along the tops of the baguettes.

Carefully transfer the baguettes to the preheated baking stone or baking sheet. Optionally, you can create steam in the oven by placing a pan of hot water on the bottom rack.

Bake the baguettes for 20-25 minutes, or until they are golden brown and sound hollow when tapped on the bottom.
Remove the baguettes from the oven and let them cool on a wire rack before slicing and serving.

Enjoy your homemade sourdough baguettes with your favorite toppings or as a side for soups, salads, or sandwiches!

Sourdough Ciabatta

Ingredients:

- 350g bread flour
- 100g whole wheat flour
- 200g active sourdough starter (100% hydration)
- 350g lukewarm water
- 8g salt

Instructions:

In a large mixing bowl, combine the active sourdough starter and lukewarm water. Mix until the starter is fully dissolved in the water.

Add the bread flour, whole wheat flour, and salt to the bowl. Mix with a wooden spoon or your hands until a shaggy dough forms.

Let the dough rest for 30 minutes to 1 hour. This step, called autolyse, allows the flour to fully hydrate and improves the dough's texture.

After the autolyse, transfer the dough to a clean, lightly floured surface. Begin the folding and stretching process. To do this, grab one edge of the dough, stretch it upwards, and then fold it over the rest of the dough. Rotate the dough and repeat this process with each side. Repeat this process several times until the dough feels smoother and more elastic.

Place the dough in a lightly oiled bowl, cover with plastic wrap or a kitchen towel, and let it rise at room temperature for about 4-6 hours, or until it has doubled in size. This step may take longer depending on the activity of your sourdough starter and the temperature of your kitchen.

Once doubled in size, gently deflate the dough and transfer it to a well-floured surface. Divide the dough into two equal portions.

Shape each portion of dough into a ciabatta shape. To do this, gently stretch the dough into a rectangle, then fold it in half lengthwise. Use your fingers to gently dimple the surface of the dough.

Place the shaped ciabatta loaves on a well-floured surface or a couche (a cloth used for proofing bread). Cover with a kitchen towel and let them rise for another 1-2 hours, or until they have visibly expanded.

Meanwhile, preheat your oven to 450°F (230°C) and place a baking stone or upside-down baking sheet in the oven to preheat.

Just before baking, carefully transfer the risen ciabatta loaves to the preheated baking stone or baking sheet.
Optionally, you can create steam in the oven by placing a pan of hot water on the bottom rack.
Bake the ciabatta loaves for 20-25 minutes, or until they are golden brown and sound hollow when tapped on the bottom.
Remove the ciabatta loaves from the oven and let them cool on a wire rack before slicing and serving.

Enjoy your homemade sourdough ciabatta with olive oil, balsamic vinegar, or your favorite toppings!

Sourdough Focaccia

Ingredients:

- 350g bread flour
- 100g whole wheat flour
- 250g active sourdough starter (100% hydration)
- 300g lukewarm water
- 8g salt
- 2-3 tablespoons olive oil
- Coarse sea salt, for topping
- Optional toppings: fresh herbs (rosemary, thyme), cherry tomatoes, olives, garlic cloves, etc.

Instructions:

In a large mixing bowl, combine the active sourdough starter and lukewarm water. Mix until the starter is fully dissolved in the water.

Add the bread flour, whole wheat flour, and salt to the bowl. Mix with a wooden spoon or your hands until a shaggy dough forms.

Let the dough rest for 30 minutes to 1 hour. This step, called autolyse, allows the flour to fully hydrate and improves the dough's texture.

After the autolyse, transfer the dough to a clean, lightly oiled bowl. Cover with plastic wrap or a kitchen towel and let it rise at room temperature for about 4-6 hours, or until it has doubled in size. This step may take longer depending on the activity of your sourdough starter and the temperature of your kitchen.

Once doubled in size, gently deflate the dough and transfer it to a well-oiled baking sheet or a baking pan. Using your fingertips, gently press and stretch the dough to fit the size of the pan. The dough should be about 1 inch thick.

Cover the pan with plastic wrap or a kitchen towel and let the dough rise for another 1-2 hours, or until it has visibly expanded.

Preheat your oven to 425°F (220°C).

Once the dough has risen, use your fingertips to make dimples all over the surface of the dough. Drizzle olive oil over the top of the dough, allowing it to pool in the dimples.

Sprinkle coarse sea salt over the top of the dough. Add any optional toppings, such as fresh herbs, cherry tomatoes, olives, or garlic cloves.

Bake the focaccia in the preheated oven for 20-25 minutes, or until it is golden brown and crisp on the outside.

Remove the focaccia from the oven and let it cool slightly before slicing and serving.

Enjoy your homemade sourdough focaccia warm with your favorite dips, or use it as a base for sandwiches and bruschetta!

Sourdough Sandwich Bread

Ingredients:

- 400g bread flour
- 100g whole wheat flour
- 250g active sourdough starter (100% hydration)
- 250g lukewarm water
- 10g salt
- 2 tablespoons honey or sugar (optional)

Instructions:

In a large mixing bowl, combine the active sourdough starter and lukewarm water. Mix until the starter is fully dissolved in the water. If desired, you can also add honey or sugar at this stage for added sweetness.

Add the bread flour, whole wheat flour, and salt to the bowl. Mix with a wooden spoon or your hands until a shaggy dough forms.

Let the dough rest for 30 minutes to 1 hour. This step, called autolyse, allows the flour to fully hydrate and improves the dough's texture.

After the autolyse, transfer the dough to a clean, lightly oiled bowl. Cover with plastic wrap or a kitchen towel and let it rise at room temperature for about 4-6 hours, or until it has doubled in size. This step may take longer depending on the activity of your sourdough starter and the temperature of your kitchen.

Once doubled in size, gently deflate the dough and transfer it to a lightly floured surface. Shape the dough into a loaf shape that will fit your bread pan.

Place the shaped dough into a lightly greased bread pan. Cover with plastic wrap or a kitchen towel and let it rise for another 1-2 hours, or until it has visibly expanded and fills the pan.

Preheat your oven to 375°F (190°C) while the dough is rising.

Once the dough has risen, remove the plastic wrap or kitchen towel and transfer the bread pan to the preheated oven.

Bake the sourdough sandwich bread for 30-35 minutes, or until it is golden brown on top and sounds hollow when tapped on the bottom.

Remove the bread from the oven and let it cool in the pan for a few minutes before transferring it to a wire rack to cool completely.

Once cooled, slice the sourdough sandwich bread and enjoy it for sandwiches, toast, or any other use!

This sourdough sandwich bread recipe yields a soft and flavorful loaf that is perfect for everyday sandwiches or toasting. Adjust the sweetness by adding more or less honey or sugar according to your taste preferences.

Sourdough Dinner Rolls

Ingredients:

- 350g bread flour
- 100g whole wheat flour
- 250g active sourdough starter (100% hydration)
- 200g lukewarm water
- 50g unsalted butter, softened
- 1 large egg
- 10g sugar
- 8g salt
- Additional melted butter for brushing (optional)

Instructions:

In a large mixing bowl, combine the active sourdough starter, lukewarm water, softened butter, egg, and sugar. Mix until well combined.

Add the bread flour, whole wheat flour, and salt to the bowl. Mix with a wooden spoon or your hands until a shaggy dough forms.

Transfer the dough to a clean, lightly floured surface. Knead the dough for about 10-15 minutes until it becomes smooth and elastic.

Place the dough in a lightly oiled bowl, cover with plastic wrap or a kitchen towel, and let it rise at room temperature for about 4-6 hours, or until it has doubled in size. This step may take longer depending on the activity of your sourdough starter and the temperature of your kitchen.

Once doubled in size, gently deflate the dough and divide it into 12 equal portions. Shape each portion into a ball and place them in a greased 9x13-inch baking dish, spaced evenly apart.

Cover the baking dish with plastic wrap or a kitchen towel and let the rolls rise for another 1-2 hours, or until they have visibly expanded and are touching each other.

Meanwhile, preheat your oven to 375°F (190°C).

Once the rolls have risen, remove the plastic wrap or kitchen towel and bake them in the preheated oven for 20-25 minutes, or until they are golden brown on top and sound hollow when tapped on the bottom.

Remove the rolls from the oven and brush the tops with melted butter, if desired. Let the rolls cool slightly in the baking dish before serving.

Enjoy your homemade sourdough dinner rolls warm with butter or as a side dish for your favorite meals!

Sourdough English Muffins

Ingredients:

- 250g bread flour
- 100g whole wheat flour
- 200g active sourdough starter (100% hydration)
- 180ml lukewarm milk
- 15g unsalted butter, softened
- 5g sugar
- 5g salt
- Cornmeal or semolina flour, for dusting

Instructions:

In a large mixing bowl, combine the active sourdough starter, lukewarm milk, softened butter, and sugar. Mix until well combined.

Add the bread flour, whole wheat flour, and salt to the bowl. Mix with a wooden spoon or your hands until a shaggy dough forms.

Transfer the dough to a clean, lightly floured surface. Knead the dough for about 10-15 minutes until it becomes smooth and elastic.

Place the dough in a lightly oiled bowl, cover with plastic wrap or a kitchen towel, and let it rise at room temperature for about 4-6 hours, or until it has doubled in size. This step may take longer depending on the activity of your sourdough starter and the temperature of your kitchen.

Once doubled in size, gently deflate the dough and transfer it to a lightly floured surface. Roll out the dough to a thickness of about 1/2 inch.

Use a round cutter or a glass to cut out circles from the dough. Place the circles on a baking sheet dusted with cornmeal or semolina flour.

Cover the baking sheet with plastic wrap or a kitchen towel and let the muffins rise for another 1-2 hours, or until they have visibly expanded.

Heat a non-stick skillet or griddle over medium-low heat. Cook the muffins for about 5-7 minutes on each side, or until they are golden brown and cooked through.

Remove the muffins from the skillet and let them cool on a wire rack.

Once cooled, use a fork to split the muffins in half. Toast them and serve with butter, jam, or your favorite toppings.

Enjoy your homemade sourdough English muffins for breakfast or as a snack!

Sourdough Cinnamon Raisin Bread

Ingredients:

- 400g bread flour
- 100g whole wheat flour
- 250g active sourdough starter (100% hydration)
- 250g lukewarm water
- 100g raisins
- 50g sugar
- 50g unsalted butter, softened
- 10g salt
- 2 teaspoons ground cinnamon

Instructions:

In a small bowl, soak the raisins in warm water for about 10 minutes to plump them up. Drain and set aside.
In a large mixing bowl, combine the active sourdough starter, lukewarm water, softened butter, and sugar. Mix until well combined.
Add the bread flour, whole wheat flour, salt, and ground cinnamon to the bowl. Mix with a wooden spoon or your hands until a shaggy dough forms.
Add the drained raisins to the dough and knead until they are evenly distributed.
Transfer the dough to a clean, lightly oiled bowl. Cover with plastic wrap or a kitchen towel and let it rise at room temperature for about 4-6 hours, or until it has doubled in size. This step may take longer depending on the activity of your sourdough starter and the temperature of your kitchen.
Once doubled in size, gently deflate the dough and transfer it to a lightly floured surface. Shape the dough into a loaf and place it in a greased loaf pan.
Cover the loaf pan with plastic wrap or a kitchen towel and let the dough rise for another 1-2 hours, or until it has visibly expanded and fills the pan.
Meanwhile, preheat your oven to 375°F (190°C).
Once the dough has risen, bake the bread in the preheated oven for 35-40 minutes, or until it is golden brown on top and sounds hollow when tapped on the bottom.
Remove the bread from the oven and let it cool in the pan for a few minutes before transferring it to a wire rack to cool completely.

Once cooled, slice the sourdough cinnamon raisin bread and enjoy it toasted with butter or your favorite spreads!

This homemade sourdough cinnamon raisin bread is perfect for breakfast or as a snack. The combination of sweet raisins and warm cinnamon makes it irresistible!

Sourdough Walnut Bread

Ingredients:

- 400g bread flour
- 100g whole wheat flour
- 250g active sourdough starter (100% hydration)
- 250g lukewarm water
- 100g chopped walnuts
- 10g salt

Instructions:

In a large mixing bowl, combine the active sourdough starter and lukewarm water. Mix until the starter is fully dissolved in the water.
Add the bread flour, whole wheat flour, and salt to the bowl. Mix with a wooden spoon or your hands until a shaggy dough forms.
Transfer the dough to a clean, lightly floured surface. Knead the dough for about 10-15 minutes until it becomes smooth and elastic.
Place the dough in a lightly oiled bowl, cover with plastic wrap or a kitchen towel, and let it rise at room temperature for about 4-6 hours, or until it has doubled in size. This step may take longer depending on the activity of your sourdough starter and the temperature of your kitchen.
Once doubled in size, gently deflate the dough and transfer it to a lightly floured surface. Sprinkle the chopped walnuts over the dough and gently knead them into the dough until evenly distributed.
Shape the dough into a loaf and place it in a greased loaf pan.
Cover the loaf pan with plastic wrap or a kitchen towel and let the dough rise for another 1-2 hours, or until it has visibly expanded and fills the pan.
Meanwhile, preheat your oven to 375°F (190°C).
Once the dough has risen, bake the bread in the preheated oven for 35-40 minutes, or until it is golden brown on top and sounds hollow when tapped on the bottom.
Remove the bread from the oven and let it cool in the pan for a few minutes before transferring it to a wire rack to cool completely.
Once cooled, slice the sourdough walnut bread and enjoy it toasted with butter or your favorite spreads!

This homemade sourdough walnut bread is perfect for adding a nutty flavor and crunchy texture to your sandwiches or enjoying on its own.

Sourdough Olive Bread

Ingredients:

- 400g bread flour
- 100g whole wheat flour
- 250g active sourdough starter (100% hydration)
- 250g lukewarm water
- 150g pitted and chopped olives (green or black)
- 10g salt

Instructions:

In a large mixing bowl, combine the active sourdough starter and lukewarm water. Mix until the starter is fully dissolved in the water.
Add the bread flour, whole wheat flour, and salt to the bowl. Mix with a wooden spoon or your hands until a shaggy dough forms.
Transfer the dough to a clean, lightly floured surface. Knead the dough for about 10-15 minutes until it becomes smooth and elastic.
Place the dough in a lightly oiled bowl, cover with plastic wrap or a kitchen towel, and let it rise at room temperature for about 4-6 hours, or until it has doubled in size. This step may take longer depending on the activity of your sourdough starter and the temperature of your kitchen.
Once doubled in size, gently deflate the dough and transfer it to a lightly floured surface. Sprinkle the chopped olives over the dough and gently knead them into the dough until evenly distributed.
Shape the dough into a loaf and place it in a greased loaf pan or on a baking sheet lined with parchment paper.
Cover the loaf pan or baking sheet with plastic wrap or a kitchen towel and let the dough rise for another 1-2 hours, or until it has visibly expanded.
Meanwhile, preheat your oven to 375°F (190°C).
Once the dough has risen, slash the top of the loaf with a sharp knife or razor blade to create steam vents. This helps the bread rise evenly in the oven.
Bake the bread in the preheated oven for 35-40 minutes, or until it is golden brown on top and sounds hollow when tapped on the bottom.
Remove the bread from the oven and let it cool on a wire rack before slicing and serving.

Enjoy your homemade sourdough olive bread with a Mediterranean twist! It's perfect for serving alongside soups, salads, or as a flavorful base for sandwiches.

Sourdough Jalapeno Cheddar Bread

Ingredients:

- 400g bread flour
- 100g whole wheat flour
- 250g active sourdough starter (100% hydration)
- 250g lukewarm water
- 100g shredded cheddar cheese
- 2-3 jalapeños, seeded and finely chopped
- 10g salt

Instructions:

In a large mixing bowl, combine the active sourdough starter and lukewarm water. Mix until the starter is fully dissolved in the water.

Add the bread flour, whole wheat flour, and salt to the bowl. Mix with a wooden spoon or your hands until a shaggy dough forms.

Transfer the dough to a clean, lightly floured surface. Knead the dough for about 10-15 minutes until it becomes smooth and elastic.

Place the dough in a lightly oiled bowl, cover with plastic wrap or a kitchen towel, and let it rise at room temperature for about 4-6 hours, or until it has doubled in size. This step may take longer depending on the activity of your sourdough starter and the temperature of your kitchen.

Once doubled in size, gently deflate the dough and transfer it to a lightly floured surface. Sprinkle the shredded cheddar cheese and chopped jalapeños over the dough. Gently knead them into the dough until evenly distributed.

Shape the dough into a loaf and place it in a greased loaf pan or on a baking sheet lined with parchment paper.

Cover the loaf pan or baking sheet with plastic wrap or a kitchen towel and let the dough rise for another 1-2 hours, or until it has visibly expanded.

Meanwhile, preheat your oven to 375°F (190°C).

Once the dough has risen, slash the top of the loaf with a sharp knife or razor blade to create steam vents. This helps the bread rise evenly in the oven.

Bake the bread in the preheated oven for 35-40 minutes, or until it is golden brown on top and sounds hollow when tapped on the bottom.

Remove the bread from the oven and let it cool on a wire rack before slicing and serving.

Enjoy your homemade sourdough jalapeño cheddar bread with a spicy kick! It's perfect for adding extra flavor to sandwiches or serving alongside soups and chili.

Sourdough Pumpernickel Bread

Ingredients:

- 250g bread flour
- 250g rye flour
- 200g active sourdough starter (100% hydration)
- 300g lukewarm water
- 50g molasses
- 10g cocoa powder
- 10g salt
- 1 tablespoon caraway seeds (optional)

Instructions:

In a large mixing bowl, combine the active sourdough starter and lukewarm water. Stir until the starter is fully dissolved in the water.
Add the bread flour, rye flour, molasses, cocoa powder, salt, and caraway seeds (if using) to the bowl. Mix until a shaggy dough forms.
Knead the dough on a lightly floured surface for about 10-15 minutes, or until it becomes smooth and elastic.
Place the dough in a lightly oiled bowl, cover with plastic wrap or a kitchen towel, and let it rise at room temperature for about 4-6 hours, or until it has doubled in size. This step may take longer depending on the activity of your sourdough starter and the temperature of your kitchen.
Once doubled in size, gently deflate the dough and shape it into a loaf. Place the loaf in a greased loaf pan or on a baking sheet lined with parchment paper.
Cover the loaf with plastic wrap or a kitchen towel and let it rise for another 1-2 hours, or until it has visibly expanded.
Meanwhile, preheat your oven to 375°F (190°C).
Once the dough has risen, bake the bread in the preheated oven for 40-45 minutes, or until it is dark brown and sounds hollow when tapped on the bottom. Remove the bread from the oven and let it cool on a wire rack before slicing and serving.

Enjoy your homemade sourdough pumpernickel bread with your favorite spreads or as a hearty addition to sandwiches and soups!

Sourdough Challah

Ingredients:

- 400g bread flour
- 100g whole wheat flour
- 250g active sourdough starter (100% hydration)
- 2 large eggs
- 75g honey or sugar
- 60ml lukewarm water
- 50ml vegetable oil
- 8g salt
- 1 egg yolk (for egg wash)
- Sesame seeds or poppy seeds (optional, for topping)

Instructions:

In a large mixing bowl, combine the active sourdough starter, lukewarm water, honey (or sugar), vegetable oil, and eggs. Mix until well combined.
Add the bread flour, whole wheat flour, and salt to the bowl. Mix with a wooden spoon or your hands until a shaggy dough forms.
Transfer the dough to a clean, lightly floured surface. Knead the dough for about 10-15 minutes until it becomes smooth and elastic.
Place the dough in a lightly oiled bowl, cover with plastic wrap or a kitchen towel, and let it rise at room temperature for about 4-6 hours, or until it has doubled in size. This step may take longer depending on the activity of your sourdough starter and the temperature of your kitchen.
Once doubled in size, gently deflate the dough and divide it into three equal portions.
Roll each portion of dough into a long rope, about 16-18 inches in length.
Place the ropes side by side and pinch the top ends together. Braid the ropes together, then pinch the bottom ends and tuck them under the loaf.
Transfer the braided loaf to a baking sheet lined with parchment paper. Cover with plastic wrap or a kitchen towel and let it rise for another 1-2 hours, or until it has visibly expanded.
Meanwhile, preheat your oven to 375°F (190°C).

Once the dough has risen, beat the egg yolk with a tablespoon of water to make an egg wash. Brush the egg wash over the top of the loaf. Optionally, sprinkle sesame seeds or poppy seeds over the top.

Bake the challah in the preheated oven for 25-30 minutes, or until it is golden brown and sounds hollow when tapped on the bottom.

Remove the challah from the oven and let it cool on a wire rack before slicing and serving.

Enjoy your homemade sourdough challah as a delicious addition to your Shabbat or holiday table!

Sourdough Brioche

Ingredients:

- 300g bread flour
- 200g all-purpose flour
- 100g active sourdough starter (100% hydration)
- 4 large eggs (at room temperature)
- 100g sugar
- 150g unsalted butter (at room temperature, cut into small pieces)
- 60ml lukewarm milk
- 5g salt

Instructions:

Activate the Starter: Make sure your sourdough starter is active and bubbly. If it's been refrigerated, you may need to feed it and let it sit at room temperature for a few hours before using it in this recipe.

Mixing the Dough: In a large mixing bowl or the bowl of a stand mixer, combine the active sourdough starter, lukewarm milk, sugar, and eggs. Mix until well combined.

Incorporate Flour: Gradually add the bread flour, all-purpose flour, and salt to the bowl, mixing until a rough dough forms.

Kneading: If using a stand mixer, switch to a dough hook attachment and knead the dough on low speed for about 5-7 minutes until it starts to come together. Then, add the softened butter, a few pieces at a time, mixing until fully incorporated before adding more. Continue kneading for another 10-15 minutes until the dough becomes smooth, elastic, and slightly tacky. If kneading by hand, knead the dough on a lightly floured surface for about 20-25 minutes.

Bulk Fermentation: Transfer the dough to a lightly oiled bowl, cover with plastic wrap or a kitchen towel, and let it rise at room temperature for about 4-6 hours, or until it has doubled in size. Alternatively, you can refrigerate the dough overnight for a slower fermentation.

Shaping: After the bulk fermentation, gently deflate the dough and divide it into equal portions. Shape each portion into balls or into the desired brioche shape (e.g., loaves, rolls, etc.).

Final Proofing: Place the shaped dough onto baking trays lined with parchment paper or into greased brioche molds. Cover with plastic wrap or a kitchen towel and let them proof at room temperature for another 2-3 hours, or until they have doubled in size and are puffy.

Preheat Oven: Preheat your oven to 375°F (190°C) during the final stages of proofing.

Baking: Once the dough has finished proofing, bake the brioche in the preheated oven for 20-25 minutes, or until they are golden brown and sound hollow when tapped on the bottom. If making larger loaves, they may need a bit longer baking time.

Cooling: Remove the brioche from the oven and let them cool on a wire rack for a few minutes before serving. Enjoy your delicious homemade Sourdough Brioche!

Making Sourdough Brioche requires time and patience, but the end result is well worth it. This rich and buttery bread is perfect for special occasions or as a treat for breakfast or brunch.

Sourdough Pretzels

Ingredients:

- 250g active sourdough starter (100% hydration)
- 375g bread flour
- 10g sugar
- 8g salt
- 1 tablespoon olive oil
- 200ml lukewarm water
- Coarse salt or pretzel salt, for topping
- Baking soda bath (1/4 cup baking soda dissolved in 4 cups of water)

Instructions:

Prepare the Dough:
- In a large mixing bowl, combine the active sourdough starter, lukewarm water, sugar, and olive oil. Mix until well combined.
- Add the bread flour and salt to the bowl. Mix until a shaggy dough forms.
- Transfer the dough to a lightly floured surface and knead for about 5-10 minutes until the dough becomes smooth and elastic.

Bulk Fermentation:
- Place the dough in a lightly oiled bowl, cover it with plastic wrap or a kitchen towel, and let it rise at room temperature for about 4-6 hours, or until it has doubled in size.

Shaping:
- Once the dough has doubled in size, turn it out onto a lightly floured surface. Divide the dough into equal-sized portions, depending on how large you want your pretzels.
- Roll each portion of dough into a long rope, about 18-20 inches in length. Shape the rope into a pretzel shape by forming a U-shape, then crossing the ends over each other and pressing them down onto the bottom of the U.

Baking Soda Bath:
- Preheat your oven to 425°F (220°C) and line a baking sheet with parchment paper.
- In a large pot, bring the baking soda and water to a boil. Once boiling, carefully lower each pretzel into the bath and let it simmer for about 30

seconds on each side. Remove the pretzels from the bath using a slotted spoon and place them on the prepared baking sheet.

Baking:
- Sprinkle coarse salt or pretzel salt over the tops of the pretzels.
- Bake the pretzels in the preheated oven for 12-15 minutes, or until they are golden brown and crisp on the outside.

Cooling and Serving:
- Remove the pretzels from the oven and let them cool on a wire rack for a few minutes before serving.
- Enjoy your homemade Sourdough Pretzels warm with mustard, cheese sauce, or any of your favorite dips!

These sourdough pretzels will have a slightly tangy flavor and a chewy texture, making them a delicious snack or appetizer for any occasion. Adjust the toppings and seasonings to your preference for a personalized touch.

Sourdough Bagels

Ingredients:

- 250g active sourdough starter (100% hydration)
- 500g bread flour
- 10g salt
- 15g sugar or honey
- 250ml lukewarm water
- 1 tablespoon baking soda (for boiling)
- Toppings of your choice (e.g., sesame seeds, poppy seeds, everything bagel seasoning, etc.)

Instructions:

Prepare the Dough:
- In a large mixing bowl, combine the active sourdough starter, lukewarm water, and sugar (or honey). Stir until the starter is fully dissolved.
- Add the bread flour and salt to the bowl. Mix until a shaggy dough forms.
- Turn the dough out onto a lightly floured surface and knead for about 10 minutes until the dough becomes smooth and elastic.

First Rise:
- Place the dough in a lightly oiled bowl, cover it with plastic wrap or a kitchen towel, and let it rise at room temperature for about 4-6 hours, or until it has doubled in size.

Shaping:
- Once the dough has doubled in size, turn it out onto a clean surface and divide it into equal-sized portions, usually around 8-10 pieces.
- Roll each portion of dough into a ball. Then, using your thumbs, poke a hole through the center of each ball and gently stretch it into a bagel shape. The hole should be about 1-2 inches in diameter.

Second Rise:
- Place the shaped bagels on a lightly floured surface or a baking sheet lined with parchment paper. Cover them with plastic wrap or a kitchen towel and let them rise for another 30-60 minutes.

Preheat Oven:
- Preheat your oven to 425°F (220°C). Bring a large pot of water to a boil and add the baking soda.

Boiling:
- Once the water is boiling, carefully lower a few bagels into the pot using a slotted spoon or spatula. Boil them for about 1 minute on each side, then remove them and place them back on the baking sheet.

Topping:
- If desired, sprinkle your chosen toppings over the boiled bagels while they are still wet. This will help the toppings adhere.

Baking:
- Bake the bagels in the preheated oven for 20-25 minutes, or until they are golden brown and have a slightly crispy crust.

Cooling and Serving:
- Remove the bagels from the oven and let them cool on a wire rack for a few minutes before serving.
- Enjoy your homemade Sourdough Bagels toasted with cream cheese, smoked salmon, or your favorite toppings!

These sourdough bagels are perfect for breakfast, brunch, or anytime you're craving a delicious and satisfying treat. Feel free to customize them with different toppings or add-ins to suit your taste preferences.

Sourdough Pizza Crust

Ingredients:

- 250g active sourdough starter (100% hydration)
- 300g bread flour
- 150g all-purpose flour
- 10g salt
- 15g olive oil
- 180ml lukewarm water

Instructions:

Prepare the Dough:
- In a large mixing bowl, combine the active sourdough starter, lukewarm water, and olive oil. Stir until the starter is fully dissolved.
- Add the bread flour, all-purpose flour, and salt to the bowl. Mix until a shaggy dough forms.

Kneading:
- Transfer the dough to a clean, lightly floured surface. Knead the dough for about 5-10 minutes until it becomes smooth and elastic.

First Rise:
- Place the dough in a lightly oiled bowl, cover it with plastic wrap or a kitchen towel, and let it rise at room temperature for about 4-6 hours, or until it has doubled in size.

Shaping:
- Once the dough has doubled in size, turn it out onto a clean surface and divide it into the desired number of pizza crusts.
- Shape each portion of dough into a ball and then flatten it into a disk. Use your hands or a rolling pin to stretch and shape the dough into your desired pizza size and thickness.

Second Rise:
- Place the shaped pizza crusts on a lightly floured surface or a baking sheet lined with parchment paper. Cover them with plastic wrap or a kitchen towel and let them rise for another 1-2 hours.

Preheat Oven:

- Preheat your oven to the highest temperature it can go, typically around 500°F to 550°F (260°C to 290°C). If you have a pizza stone or baking steel, place it in the oven to preheat as well.

Topping and Baking:
- Once the oven is preheated and the pizza crusts have finished rising, top the crusts with your favorite pizza sauce, cheese, and toppings.
- Carefully transfer the topped pizzas to the preheated pizza stone or baking sheet.
- Bake the pizzas in the preheated oven for 10-15 minutes, or until the crust is golden brown and the cheese is bubbly and melted.

Cooling and Serving:
- Remove the pizzas from the oven and let them cool on a wire rack for a few minutes before slicing and serving.
- Enjoy your homemade Sourdough Pizza with your favorite toppings!

These sourdough pizza crusts will have a deliciously tangy flavor and a chewy texture that pairs perfectly with a variety of toppings. Experiment with different toppings and sauces to create your own unique pizza creations!

Sourdough Flatbread

Ingredients:

- 250g active sourdough starter (100% hydration)
- 250g bread flour
- 5g salt
- 60ml lukewarm water
- 15ml olive oil (plus extra for brushing)
- Optional toppings: herbs, garlic, cheese, seeds, etc.

Instructions:

Prepare the Dough:
- In a large mixing bowl, combine the active sourdough starter, lukewarm water, and olive oil. Stir until the starter is fully dissolved.
- Add the bread flour and salt to the bowl. Mix until a shaggy dough forms.

Kneading:
- Transfer the dough to a clean, lightly floured surface. Knead the dough for about 5-10 minutes until it becomes smooth and elastic.

First Rise:
- Place the dough in a lightly oiled bowl, cover it with plastic wrap or a kitchen towel, and let it rise at room temperature for about 4-6 hours, or until it has doubled in size.

Shaping:
- Once the dough has doubled in size, turn it out onto a clean surface and divide it into smaller portions, depending on how many flatbreads you want to make.
- Roll each portion of dough into a ball and then flatten it into a disk. Use a rolling pin to roll out each disk into a thin flatbread, about 1/4 inch thick.

Second Rise (Optional):
- Place the rolled-out flatbreads on a lightly floured surface or a baking sheet lined with parchment paper. Cover them with plastic wrap or a kitchen towel and let them rise for another 30-60 minutes for a lighter texture.

Preheat Oven:
- Preheat your oven to 400°F (200°C).

Topping (Optional):

- If desired, brush the tops of the flatbreads with olive oil and sprinkle with your choice of toppings, such as herbs, garlic, cheese, seeds, etc.

Baking:
- Place the flatbreads on a baking sheet or directly on a preheated pizza stone or baking steel.
- Bake in the preheated oven for 10-15 minutes, or until the flatbreads are golden brown and slightly crispy around the edges.

Cooling and Serving:
- Remove the flatbreads from the oven and let them cool on a wire rack for a few minutes before serving.
- Enjoy your homemade Sourdough Flatbreads warm with your favorite dips, spreads, or as a side to soups and salads!

These sourdough flatbreads are deliciously tangy and versatile, making them perfect for serving alongside a variety of dishes or as a base for pizzas or sandwiches. Experiment with different toppings and flavors to customize them to your liking!

Sourdough Crackers

Ingredients:

- 200g sourdough discard (unfed, 100% hydration)
- 100g all-purpose flour (plus extra for dusting)
- 25g whole wheat flour (optional, for added flavor)
- 25g olive oil (or melted butter)
- 1/2 teaspoon salt
- Herbs, spices, or other seasonings of your choice (optional, for flavor)

Instructions:

Prepare the Dough:
- In a mixing bowl, combine the sourdough discard, all-purpose flour, whole wheat flour (if using), olive oil (or melted butter), and salt. Mix until the ingredients come together into a dough.
- If desired, add herbs, spices, or other seasonings to flavor the dough. Mix until evenly distributed.

Knead and Rest:
- Turn the dough out onto a lightly floured surface and knead it briefly until it forms a smooth ball. Avoid overworking the dough.
- Wrap the dough in plastic wrap and let it rest at room temperature for about 30 minutes. This allows the gluten to relax and makes the dough easier to roll out.

Preheat Oven:
- Preheat your oven to 350°F (175°C) and line a baking sheet with parchment paper.

Roll Out the Dough:
- After resting, unwrap the dough and place it on a lightly floured surface. Use a rolling pin to roll out the dough into a thin, even sheet. Aim for about 1/8 inch (3mm) thickness.

Cut the Crackers:
- Use a sharp knife, pizza cutter, or cookie cutter to cut the rolled-out dough into individual crackers of your desired shape and size. You can make them square, rectangular, or use a cookie cutter for fun shapes.

Prick the Crackers:

- Use a fork to prick the surface of each cracker several times. This helps prevent the crackers from puffing up too much during baking.

Bake the Crackers:
- Transfer the cut crackers to the prepared baking sheet, leaving a little space between each one.
- Bake in the preheated oven for about 15-20 minutes, or until the crackers are golden brown and crispy. Keep an eye on them towards the end of the baking time to prevent burning.

Cool and Enjoy:
- Once baked, remove the crackers from the oven and let them cool completely on a wire rack.
- Once cooled, store the sourdough crackers in an airtight container at room temperature. Enjoy them plain or with your favorite dips, cheeses, or spreads!

Feel free to experiment with different seasonings and flavorings to customize these sourdough crackers to your taste preferences. Enjoy your homemade snacks!

Sourdough Pancakes

Ingredients:

- 1 cup (240g) active sourdough starter (100% hydration)
- 1 cup (240ml) milk (any kind)
- 2 tablespoons (30ml) maple syrup or honey
- 1 large egg
- 2 tablespoons (30g) melted butter or oil
- 1 cup (125g) all-purpose flour
- 1/2 teaspoon baking soda
- 1/2 teaspoon salt

Instructions:

Prepare the Batter:
- In a mixing bowl, combine the active sourdough starter, milk, maple syrup or honey, egg, and melted butter or oil. Mix until well combined.

Add Dry Ingredients:
- Add the all-purpose flour, baking soda, and salt to the bowl. Stir until just combined. It's okay if there are a few lumps in the batter; avoid overmixing.

Rest the Batter:
- Let the batter rest for about 10-15 minutes. This allows the flour to hydrate and the leavening agents to activate.

Preheat the Griddle or Pan:
- Preheat a non-stick griddle or skillet over medium heat. If using a skillet, lightly grease it with butter or oil.

Cook the Pancakes:
- Once the griddle or skillet is hot, pour about 1/4 cup of batter onto the cooking surface for each pancake. Use the back of a spoon to spread the batter into a round shape if needed.
- Cook the pancakes for 2-3 minutes, or until bubbles form on the surface and the edges begin to look set.

Flip and Cook:
- Carefully flip the pancakes with a spatula and cook for an additional 1-2 minutes on the other side, or until golden brown and cooked through.

Repeat:

- Continue cooking the remaining batter in batches, adding more oil or butter to the skillet as needed.

Serve Warm:
- Serve the sourdough pancakes warm, topped with your favorite toppings such as maple syrup, fresh fruit, whipped cream, or nuts.

Enjoy:
- Enjoy your delicious homemade sourdough pancakes for a tasty breakfast or brunch treat!

These sourdough pancakes are fluffy, flavorful, and have a subtle tanginess from the sourdough starter. They're a wonderful way to start the day and make use of your sourdough discard. Feel free to adjust the sweetness or add extra flavorings like cinnamon or vanilla extract to customize them to your liking!

Sourdough Waffles

Ingredients:

- 1 cup (240g) active sourdough starter (100% hydration)
- 1 1/2 cups (360ml) milk (any kind)
- 2 large eggs
- 1/4 cup (50g) melted butter or oil
- 2 tablespoons (30ml) maple syrup or honey (optional, adjust to taste)
- 1 teaspoon vanilla extract (optional)
- 2 cups (250g) all-purpose flour
- 1 teaspoon baking powder
- 1/2 teaspoon baking soda
- 1/2 teaspoon salt

Instructions:

Prepare the Batter:
- In a large mixing bowl, combine the active sourdough starter, milk, eggs, melted butter or oil, maple syrup or honey (if using), and vanilla extract (if using). Mix until well combined.

Add Dry Ingredients:
- Add the all-purpose flour, baking powder, baking soda, and salt to the bowl. Stir until just combined. It's okay if there are a few lumps in the batter; avoid overmixing.

Rest the Batter:
- Let the batter rest for about 10-15 minutes. This allows the flour to hydrate and the leavening agents to activate.

Preheat the Waffle Iron:
- Preheat your waffle iron according to the manufacturer's instructions.

Cook the Waffles:
- Once the waffle iron is hot, pour an appropriate amount of batter onto the center of the preheated waffle iron, using a ladle or measuring cup. The amount will depend on the size of your waffle iron.
- Close the waffle iron and cook the waffles according to the manufacturer's instructions, until they are golden brown and crispy.

Serve Warm:

- Serve the sourdough waffles warm, topped with your favorite toppings such as maple syrup, fresh fruit, whipped cream, or nuts.

Enjoy:
- Enjoy your delicious homemade sourdough waffles for a delightful breakfast or brunch treat!

These sourdough waffles are light, fluffy, and have a subtle tanginess from the sourdough starter. They're a wonderful way to start the day and make use of your sourdough discard. Feel free to adjust the sweetness or add extra flavorings like cinnamon or lemon zest to customize them to your liking!

Sourdough French Toast

Ingredients:

- 4 slices of day-old sourdough bread (thickly sliced)
- 2 large eggs
- 1/2 cup (120ml) milk (any kind)
- 1 tablespoon maple syrup or honey
- 1/2 teaspoon vanilla extract
- 1/4 teaspoon ground cinnamon (optional)
- Butter or oil for cooking
- Toppings of your choice (such as maple syrup, fresh fruit, powdered sugar, or whipped cream)

Instructions:

Prepare the Batter:
- In a shallow dish or bowl, whisk together the eggs, milk, maple syrup or honey, vanilla extract, and ground cinnamon (if using) until well combined. This will be your French toast batter.

Soak the Bread:
- Dip each slice of sourdough bread into the batter, allowing it to soak for about 20-30 seconds on each side. Make sure the bread is evenly coated with the batter, but not overly soaked.

Cook the French Toast:
- Heat a skillet or griddle over medium heat and add a pat of butter or a drizzle of oil to grease the pan.
- Once the pan is hot, add the soaked bread slices to the pan in a single layer. Cook for 2-3 minutes on each side, or until golden brown and cooked through.
- Repeat with the remaining slices of bread, adding more butter or oil to the pan as needed.

Serve Warm:
- Once cooked, transfer the French toast to plates and serve warm.
- Top with your favorite toppings, such as maple syrup, fresh fruit, powdered sugar, or whipped cream.

Enjoy:

- Enjoy your delicious homemade sourdough French toast for a delightful breakfast or brunch treat!

Sourdough French toast has a slightly tangy flavor and a fluffy texture, making it a unique and delicious twist on the classic dish. Feel free to customize it with your favorite toppings and enjoy it as a special treat to start your day.

Sourdough Donuts

Ingredients:

For the doughnuts:

- 1 cup (240g) active sourdough starter (100% hydration)
- 1/2 cup (120ml) milk (any kind)
- 2 tablespoons (30g) unsalted butter, melted
- 1/4 cup (50g) granulated sugar
- 1 large egg
- 1 teaspoon vanilla extract
- 2 1/2 cups (310g) all-purpose flour
- 1/2 teaspoon salt
- 1/2 teaspoon ground nutmeg (optional)
- Oil for frying

For the glaze:

- 1 cup (120g) powdered sugar
- 2-3 tablespoons (30-45ml) milk or water
- 1/2 teaspoon vanilla extract

Instructions:

Prepare the Dough:
- In a large mixing bowl, combine the active sourdough starter, milk, melted butter, sugar, egg, and vanilla extract. Mix until well combined.
- Add the all-purpose flour, salt, and ground nutmeg (if using) to the bowl. Stir until a sticky dough forms.

Knead and Rest the Dough:
- Turn the dough out onto a lightly floured surface and knead it for about 5-10 minutes until it becomes smooth and elastic. Add more flour if necessary to prevent sticking.
- Place the dough in a lightly oiled bowl, cover it with plastic wrap or a kitchen towel, and let it rest at room temperature for about 1-2 hours, or until it has doubled in size.

Roll and Cut the Doughnuts:
- Once the dough has doubled in size, turn it out onto a lightly floured surface. Roll it out to a thickness of about 1/2 inch (1.3 cm).
- Use a doughnut cutter or two different-sized round cutters to cut out doughnuts and doughnut holes from the dough. Re-roll any scraps and continue cutting until all the dough is used.

Second Rise:
- Place the cut doughnuts and doughnut holes on a lightly floured baking sheet, leaving some space between them. Cover with plastic wrap or a kitchen towel and let them rise for another 30-60 minutes, or until they are puffy and have doubled in size.

Fry the Doughnuts:
- Heat oil in a deep fryer or large heavy-bottomed pot to 350°F (175°C).
- Carefully add a few doughnuts to the hot oil, being careful not to overcrowd the pot. Fry for about 1-2 minutes on each side, or until they are golden brown and cooked through.
- Use a slotted spoon or spider strainer to remove the fried doughnuts from the oil and place them on a wire rack set over a baking sheet to drain.

Make the Glaze:
- In a small bowl, whisk together the powdered sugar, milk or water, and vanilla extract until smooth. Adjust the consistency by adding more liquid if needed.

Glaze the Doughnuts:
- While the doughnuts are still warm, dip them into the glaze, turning to coat both sides. Allow any excess glaze to drip off, then return the glazed doughnuts to the wire rack to set.

Serve and Enjoy:
- Serve the sourdough doughnuts warm or at room temperature. Enjoy them as a delicious treat any time of day!

These sourdough doughnuts are sure to be a hit with friends and family. Feel free to customize them by adding different toppings or fillings, such as chocolate glaze, sprinkles, or fruit preserves. Enjoy your homemade sourdough doughnuts!

Sourdough Banana Bread

Ingredients:

- 1 cup (240g) ripe bananas, mashed (about 2-3 medium bananas)
- 1/2 cup (120g) active sourdough starter (100% hydration)
- 1/2 cup (120ml) vegetable oil or melted butter
- 2 large eggs
- 1 teaspoon vanilla extract
- 1 cup (200g) granulated sugar
- 1 3/4 cups (220g) all-purpose flour
- 1 teaspoon baking soda
- 1/2 teaspoon salt
- Optional add-ins: chopped nuts, chocolate chips, or dried fruit

Instructions:

Preheat Oven and Prepare Pan:
- Preheat your oven to 350°F (175°C). Grease and flour a 9x5-inch loaf pan, or line it with parchment paper for easy removal.

Mix Wet Ingredients:
- In a large mixing bowl, combine the mashed bananas, active sourdough starter, vegetable oil or melted butter, eggs, and vanilla extract. Mix until well combined.

Add Dry Ingredients:
- Add the granulated sugar, all-purpose flour, baking soda, and salt to the bowl. Mix until just combined. Be careful not to overmix; a few lumps are okay.

Optional Add-Ins:
- If desired, fold in chopped nuts, chocolate chips, or dried fruit until evenly distributed throughout the batter.

Transfer to Pan:
- Pour the batter into the prepared loaf pan, spreading it out evenly with a spatula.

Bake:
- Place the loaf pan in the preheated oven and bake for 50-60 minutes, or until a toothpick inserted into the center of the bread comes out clean.

Cool:

- Once baked, remove the banana bread from the oven and let it cool in the pan for about 10 minutes. Then, transfer it to a wire rack to cool completely.

Slice and Serve:
- Once cooled, slice the sourdough banana bread and serve. Enjoy it plain or with a smear of butter for a delicious treat!

Sourdough banana bread has a wonderful tangy flavor and a moist, tender crumb. It's a great way to use up ripe bananas and add a unique twist to a classic recipe. Feel free to customize it with your favorite add-ins or enjoy it as is!

Sourdough Zucchini Bread

Ingredients:

- 1 cup (240g) active sourdough starter (100% hydration)
- 2 cups (250g) grated zucchini (about 1 medium zucchini)
- 1/2 cup (120ml) vegetable oil or melted butter
- 2 large eggs
- 1 teaspoon vanilla extract
- 3/4 cup (150g) granulated sugar
- 1 3/4 cups (220g) all-purpose flour
- 1 teaspoon baking powder
- 1/2 teaspoon baking soda
- 1/2 teaspoon salt
- 1 teaspoon ground cinnamon
- Optional add-ins: chopped nuts, raisins, or chocolate chips

Instructions:

Preheat Oven and Prepare Pan:
- Preheat your oven to 350°F (175°C). Grease and flour a 9x5-inch loaf pan, or line it with parchment paper for easy removal.

Grate Zucchini:
- Grate the zucchini using a box grater. Place the grated zucchini in a clean kitchen towel and squeeze out any excess moisture.

Mix Wet Ingredients:
- In a large mixing bowl, combine the active sourdough starter, grated zucchini, vegetable oil or melted butter, eggs, and vanilla extract. Mix until well combined.

Add Dry Ingredients:
- Add the granulated sugar, all-purpose flour, baking powder, baking soda, salt, and ground cinnamon to the bowl. Mix until just combined. Be careful not to overmix; a few lumps are okay.

Optional Add-Ins:
- If desired, fold in chopped nuts, raisins, or chocolate chips until evenly distributed throughout the batter.

Transfer to Pan:

- Pour the batter into the prepared loaf pan, spreading it out evenly with a spatula.

Bake:
- Place the loaf pan in the preheated oven and bake for 50-60 minutes, or until a toothpick inserted into the center of the bread comes out clean.

Cool:
- Once baked, remove the zucchini bread from the oven and let it cool in the pan for about 10 minutes. Then, transfer it to a wire rack to cool completely.

Slice and Serve:
- Once cooled, slice the sourdough zucchini bread and serve. Enjoy it plain or with a smear of butter for a delicious treat!

Sourdough zucchini bread has a wonderful tangy flavor and a moist, tender crumb. It's a great way to use up fresh zucchini and add a unique twist to a classic recipe. Feel free to customize it with your favorite add-ins or enjoy it as is!

Sourdough Pumpkin Bread

Ingredients:

- 1 cup (240g) active sourdough starter (100% hydration)
- 1 cup (245g) pumpkin puree
- 1/2 cup (120ml) vegetable oil or melted butter
- 2 large eggs
- 1 teaspoon vanilla extract
- 3/4 cup (150g) granulated sugar
- 1 3/4 cups (220g) all-purpose flour
- 1 teaspoon baking powder
- 1/2 teaspoon baking soda
- 1/2 teaspoon salt
- 1 teaspoon ground cinnamon
- 1/2 teaspoon ground nutmeg
- 1/4 teaspoon ground cloves
- Optional add-ins: chopped nuts, raisins, or chocolate chips

Instructions:

Preheat Oven and Prepare Pan:
- Preheat your oven to 350°F (175°C). Grease and flour a 9x5-inch loaf pan, or line it with parchment paper for easy removal.

Mix Wet Ingredients:
- In a large mixing bowl, combine the active sourdough starter, pumpkin puree, vegetable oil or melted butter, eggs, and vanilla extract. Mix until well combined.

Add Dry Ingredients:
- Add the granulated sugar, all-purpose flour, baking powder, baking soda, salt, ground cinnamon, ground nutmeg, and ground cloves to the bowl. Mix until just combined. Be careful not to overmix; a few lumps are okay.

Optional Add-Ins:
- If desired, fold in chopped nuts, raisins, or chocolate chips until evenly distributed throughout the batter.

Transfer to Pan:
- Pour the batter into the prepared loaf pan, spreading it out evenly with a spatula.

Bake:

- Place the loaf pan in the preheated oven and bake for 50-60 minutes, or until a toothpick inserted into the center of the bread comes out clean.

Cool:
- Once baked, remove the pumpkin bread from the oven and let it cool in the pan for about 10 minutes. Then, transfer it to a wire rack to cool completely.

Slice and Serve:
- Once cooled, slice the sourdough pumpkin bread and serve. Enjoy it plain or with a smear of butter for a delicious treat!

Sourdough pumpkin bread has a wonderful tangy flavor and a moist, tender crumb with the delicious aroma and flavor of pumpkin and spices. It's perfect for enjoying during the fall season or any time of the year! Feel free to customize it with your favorite add-ins or enjoy it as is.

Sourdough Chocolate Chip Bread

Ingredients:

- 1 cup (240g) active sourdough starter (100% hydration)
- 3/4 cup (180ml) milk (any kind)
- 1/4 cup (60g) vegetable oil or melted butter
- 1/2 cup (100g) granulated sugar
- 1 large egg
- 1 teaspoon vanilla extract
- 2 cups (250g) all-purpose flour
- 1 teaspoon baking powder
- 1/2 teaspoon baking soda
- 1/2 teaspoon salt
- 1/2 cup (90g) chocolate chips (semi-sweet or milk chocolate)

Instructions:

Preheat Oven and Prepare Pan:
- Preheat your oven to 350°F (175°C). Grease and flour a 9x5-inch loaf pan, or line it with parchment paper for easy removal.

Mix Wet Ingredients:
- In a large mixing bowl, combine the active sourdough starter, milk, vegetable oil or melted butter, granulated sugar, egg, and vanilla extract. Mix until well combined.

Add Dry Ingredients:
- Add the all-purpose flour, baking powder, baking soda, and salt to the bowl. Mix until just combined. Be careful not to overmix; a few lumps are okay.

Fold in Chocolate Chips:
- Gently fold in the chocolate chips until evenly distributed throughout the batter.

Transfer to Pan:
- Pour the batter into the prepared loaf pan, spreading it out evenly with a spatula.

Bake:
- Place the loaf pan in the preheated oven and bake for 50-60 minutes, or until a toothpick inserted into the center of the bread comes out clean.

Cool:
- Once baked, remove the chocolate chip bread from the oven and let it cool in the pan for about 10 minutes. Then, transfer it to a wire rack to cool completely.

Slice and Serve:
- Once cooled, slice the sourdough chocolate chip bread and serve. Enjoy it plain or with a smear of butter for a delicious treat!

Sourdough chocolate chip bread has a wonderful tangy flavor from the sourdough starter, combined with the sweetness of chocolate chips. It's perfect for breakfast, brunch, or as a snack any time of the day. Feel free to customize it with additional add-ins such as nuts or dried fruit if desired. Enjoy!

Sourdough Apple Cinnamon Bread

Ingredients:

- 1 cup (240g) active sourdough starter (100% hydration)
- 3/4 cup (180ml) milk (any kind)
- 1/4 cup (60g) vegetable oil or melted butter
- 1/2 cup (100g) granulated sugar
- 1 large egg
- 1 teaspoon vanilla extract
- 2 cups (250g) all-purpose flour
- 1 teaspoon baking powder
- 1/2 teaspoon baking soda
- 1/2 teaspoon salt
- 1 teaspoon ground cinnamon
- 1 cup (about 1 medium) finely chopped apples (peeled and cored)
- Optional: 1/2 cup (90g) chopped nuts (such as walnuts or pecans)

Instructions:

Preheat Oven and Prepare Pan:
- Preheat your oven to 350°F (175°C). Grease and flour a 9x5-inch loaf pan, or line it with parchment paper for easy removal.

Mix Wet Ingredients:
- In a large mixing bowl, combine the active sourdough starter, milk, vegetable oil or melted butter, granulated sugar, egg, and vanilla extract. Mix until well combined.

Add Dry Ingredients:
- Add the all-purpose flour, baking powder, baking soda, salt, and ground cinnamon to the bowl. Mix until just combined. Be careful not to overmix; a few lumps are okay.

Fold in Apples and Nuts:
- Gently fold in the chopped apples and chopped nuts (if using) until evenly distributed throughout the batter.

Transfer to Pan:
- Pour the batter into the prepared loaf pan, spreading it out evenly with a spatula.

Bake:

- Place the loaf pan in the preheated oven and bake for 50-60 minutes, or until a toothpick inserted into the center of the bread comes out clean.

Cool:
- Once baked, remove the apple cinnamon bread from the oven and let it cool in the pan for about 10 minutes. Then, transfer it to a wire rack to cool completely.

Slice and Serve:
- Once cooled, slice the sourdough apple cinnamon bread and serve. Enjoy it plain or with a smear of butter for a delicious treat!

Sourdough apple cinnamon bread is perfect for breakfast, brunch, or as a snack any time of the day. It's moist, flavorful, and packed with the delicious combination of apples and cinnamon. Feel free to customize it with additional add-ins such as raisins or dried cranberries if desired. Enjoy!

Sourdough Lemon Poppyseed Bread

Ingredients:

- 1 cup (240g) active sourdough starter (100% hydration)
- 3/4 cup (180ml) milk (any kind)
- 1/4 cup (60ml) vegetable oil or melted butter
- Zest of 1 lemon
- 1/4 cup (60ml) freshly squeezed lemon juice
- 1/2 cup (100g) granulated sugar
- 1 large egg
- 1 teaspoon vanilla extract
- 2 cups (250g) all-purpose flour
- 1 teaspoon baking powder
- 1/2 teaspoon baking soda
- 1/2 teaspoon salt
- 2 tablespoons poppy seeds

Instructions:

Preheat Oven and Prepare Pan:
- Preheat your oven to 350°F (175°C). Grease and flour a 9x5-inch loaf pan, or line it with parchment paper for easy removal.

Mix Wet Ingredients:
- In a large mixing bowl, combine the active sourdough starter, milk, vegetable oil or melted butter, lemon zest, lemon juice, granulated sugar, egg, and vanilla extract. Mix until well combined.

Add Dry Ingredients:
- Add the all-purpose flour, baking powder, baking soda, salt, and poppy seeds to the bowl. Mix until just combined. Be careful not to overmix; a few lumps are okay.

Transfer to Pan:
- Pour the batter into the prepared loaf pan, spreading it out evenly with a spatula.

Bake:
- Place the loaf pan in the preheated oven and bake for 50-60 minutes, or until a toothpick inserted into the center of the bread comes out clean.

Cool:

- Once baked, remove the lemon poppyseed bread from the oven and let it cool in the pan for about 10 minutes. Then, transfer it to a wire rack to cool completely.

Slice and Serve:
- Once cooled, slice the sourdough lemon poppyseed bread and serve. Enjoy it plain or with a smear of butter for a delicious treat!

Sourdough lemon poppyseed bread is perfect for breakfast, brunch, or as a snack any time of the day. It's moist, flavorful, and packed with the bright, citrusy flavor of lemon and the crunch of poppy seeds. Enjoy!

Sourdough Cranberry Orange Bread

Ingredients:

- 1 cup (240g) active sourdough starter (100% hydration)
- 3/4 cup (180ml) milk (any kind)
- 1/4 cup (60ml) vegetable oil or melted butter
- Zest of 1 orange
- 1/4 cup (60ml) freshly squeezed orange juice
- 1/2 cup (100g) granulated sugar
- 1 large egg
- 1 teaspoon vanilla extract
- 2 cups (250g) all-purpose flour
- 1 teaspoon baking powder
- 1/2 teaspoon baking soda
- 1/2 teaspoon salt
- 1 cup (120g) fresh or frozen cranberries, coarsely chopped

Instructions:

Preheat Oven and Prepare Pan:
- Preheat your oven to 350°F (175°C). Grease and flour a 9x5-inch loaf pan, or line it with parchment paper for easy removal.

Mix Wet Ingredients:
- In a large mixing bowl, combine the active sourdough starter, milk, vegetable oil or melted butter, orange zest, orange juice, granulated sugar, egg, and vanilla extract. Mix until well combined.

Add Dry Ingredients:
- Add the all-purpose flour, baking powder, baking soda, and salt to the bowl. Mix until just combined. Be careful not to overmix; a few lumps are okay.

Fold in Cranberries:
- Gently fold in the chopped cranberries until evenly distributed throughout the batter.

Transfer to Pan:
- Pour the batter into the prepared loaf pan, spreading it out evenly with a spatula.

Bake:

- Place the loaf pan in the preheated oven and bake for 50-60 minutes, or until a toothpick inserted into the center of the bread comes out clean.

Cool:
- Once baked, remove the cranberry orange bread from the oven and let it cool in the pan for about 10 minutes. Then, transfer it to a wire rack to cool completely.

Slice and Serve:
- Once cooled, slice the sourdough cranberry orange bread and serve. Enjoy it plain or with a smear of butter for a delicious treat!

Sourdough cranberry orange bread is perfect for breakfast, brunch, or as a snack any time of the day. It's moist, flavorful, and packed with the bright, citrusy flavor of orange and the tartness of cranberries. Enjoy!

Sourdough Artisan Loaf with Herbs

Ingredients:

- 1 cup (240g) active sourdough starter (100% hydration)
- 1 1/2 cups (360ml) lukewarm water
- 4 cups (500g) bread flour
- 2 teaspoons salt
- 2 tablespoons chopped fresh herbs (such as rosemary, thyme, oregano, or a combination)
- Additional flour for dusting
- Cornmeal or semolina flour for dusting (optional)

Instructions:

Mix the Dough:
- In a large mixing bowl, combine the active sourdough starter and lukewarm water. Stir until the starter is dissolved in the water.
- Add the bread flour and salt to the bowl. Mix until a shaggy dough forms and all the flour is hydrated.
- Fold in the chopped fresh herbs until evenly distributed throughout the dough.

Bulk Fermentation:
- Cover the bowl with a clean kitchen towel or plastic wrap and let the dough rest at room temperature for about 4-6 hours. During this time, perform a series of stretch and folds every 30 minutes for the first 2 hours to develop gluten.

Shape the Dough:
- After the bulk fermentation, lightly flour a work surface. Carefully transfer the dough onto the floured surface.
- Gently shape the dough into a round or oval loaf, being careful not to deflate it too much.
- Place the shaped loaf onto a piece of parchment paper dusted with cornmeal or semolina flour, if using.

Final Proofing:
- Cover the shaped loaf with a clean kitchen towel and let it proof at room temperature for 1-2 hours, or until it has visibly increased in size and is puffy.

Preheat the Oven:

- About 30 minutes before the final proofing is complete, preheat your oven to 450°F (230°C). Place a Dutch oven or baking stone on the middle rack of the oven during preheating.

Score the Loaf:
- Once the oven is preheated and the dough has finished proofing, carefully score the top of the loaf with a sharp knife or bread lame to create decorative slashes.

Bake the Loaf:
- Carefully transfer the scored loaf, still on the parchment paper, into the preheated Dutch oven or onto the preheated baking stone.
- Bake the loaf covered for 20-25 minutes to create steam, then remove the lid or cover and continue baking for an additional 20-25 minutes, or until the crust is golden brown and the loaf sounds hollow when tapped on the bottom.
- Once baked, transfer the loaf to a wire rack to cool completely before slicing.

Enjoy:
- Once cooled, slice your Sourdough Artisan Loaf with Herbs and enjoy the wonderful flavors of the fresh herbs infused throughout the bread.

This sourdough bread is perfect for serving alongside soups, salads, or enjoyed on its own with a smear of butter. The aromatic herbs add a beautiful flavor and aroma to the loaf, making it a delightful addition to any meal.

Sourdough Seeded Bread

Ingredients:

- 1 cup (240g) active sourdough starter (100% hydration)
- 1 1/2 cups (360ml) lukewarm water
- 4 cups (500g) bread flour
- 2 teaspoons salt
- 1/4 cup (40g) mixed seeds (such as sesame seeds, sunflower seeds, pumpkin seeds, flaxseeds, chia seeds, etc.)
- Additional seeds for topping (optional)

Instructions:

Mix the Dough:
- In a large mixing bowl, combine the active sourdough starter and lukewarm water. Stir until the starter is dissolved in the water.
- Add the bread flour and salt to the bowl. Mix until a shaggy dough forms and all the flour is hydrated.
- Fold in the mixed seeds until evenly distributed throughout the dough.

Bulk Fermentation:
- Cover the bowl with a clean kitchen towel or plastic wrap and let the dough rest at room temperature for about 4-6 hours. During this time, perform a series of stretch and folds every 30 minutes for the first 2 hours to develop gluten.

Shape the Dough:
- After the bulk fermentation, lightly flour a work surface. Carefully transfer the dough onto the floured surface.
- Gently shape the dough into a round or oval loaf, being careful not to deflate it too much.

Final Proofing:
- Place the shaped loaf onto a piece of parchment paper. Cover the loaf with a clean kitchen towel and let it proof at room temperature for 1-2 hours, or until it has visibly increased in size and is puffy.

Preheat the Oven:
- About 30 minutes before the final proofing is complete, preheat your oven to 450°F (230°C). Place a Dutch oven or baking stone on the middle rack of the oven during preheating.

Score and Seed the Loaf:
- Once the oven is preheated and the dough has finished proofing, carefully score the top of the loaf with a sharp knife or bread lame to create decorative slashes.
- If desired, sprinkle additional seeds on top of the loaf and gently press them into the surface.

Bake the Loaf:
- Carefully transfer the scored and seeded loaf, still on the parchment paper, into the preheated Dutch oven or onto the preheated baking stone.
- Bake the loaf covered for 20-25 minutes to create steam, then remove the lid or cover and continue baking for an additional 20-25 minutes, or until the crust is golden brown and the loaf sounds hollow when tapped on the bottom.

Cool and Enjoy:
- Once baked, transfer the loaf to a wire rack to cool completely before slicing. Enjoy your Sourdough Seeded Bread with your favorite toppings or spreads!

This Sourdough Seeded Bread is packed with flavor and texture from the variety of seeds incorporated into the dough. It's perfect for sandwiches, toast, or enjoyed on its own as a delicious and nutritious snack.

Sourdough Multigrain Bread

Ingredients:

- 1 cup (240g) active sourdough starter (100% hydration)
- 1 1/2 cups (360ml) lukewarm water
- 4 cups (500g) bread flour
- 1/2 cup (70g) whole wheat flour
- 1/4 cup (30g) rolled oats
- 1/4 cup (30g) cornmeal
- 1/4 cup (30g) wheat germ
- 1/4 cup (40g) mixed seeds (such as sesame seeds, sunflower seeds, pumpkin seeds, flaxseeds, chia seeds, etc.)
- 2 teaspoons salt

Instructions:

Mix the Dough:
- In a large mixing bowl, combine the active sourdough starter and lukewarm water. Stir until the starter is dissolved in the water.
- Add the bread flour, whole wheat flour, rolled oats, cornmeal, wheat germ, mixed seeds, and salt to the bowl. Mix until a shaggy dough forms and all the flour is hydrated.

Bulk Fermentation:
- Cover the bowl with a clean kitchen towel or plastic wrap and let the dough rest at room temperature for about 4-6 hours. During this time, perform a series of stretch and folds every 30 minutes for the first 2 hours to develop gluten.

Shape the Dough:
- After the bulk fermentation, lightly flour a work surface. Carefully transfer the dough onto the floured surface.
- Gently shape the dough into a round or oval loaf, being careful not to deflate it too much.

Final Proofing:
- Place the shaped loaf onto a piece of parchment paper. Cover the loaf with a clean kitchen towel and let it proof at room temperature for 1-2 hours, or until it has visibly increased in size and is puffy.

Preheat the Oven:

- About 30 minutes before the final proofing is complete, preheat your oven to 450°F (230°C). Place a Dutch oven or baking stone on the middle rack of the oven during preheating.

Score the Loaf:
- Once the oven is preheated and the dough has finished proofing, carefully score the top of the loaf with a sharp knife or bread lame to create decorative slashes.

Bake the Loaf:
- Carefully transfer the scored loaf, still on the parchment paper, into the preheated Dutch oven or onto the preheated baking stone.
- Bake the loaf covered for 20-25 minutes to create steam, then remove the lid or cover and continue baking for an additional 20-25 minutes, or until the crust is golden brown and the loaf sounds hollow when tapped on the bottom.

Cool and Enjoy:
- Once baked, transfer the loaf to a wire rack to cool completely before slicing. Enjoy your Sourdough Multigrain Bread with your favorite toppings or spreads!

This Sourdough Multigrain Bread is packed with flavor and nutrition from the variety of grains and seeds incorporated into the dough. It's perfect for sandwiches, toast, or enjoyed on its own as a delicious and hearty snack.

Sourdough Spelt Bread

Ingredients:

- 1 cup (240g) active sourdough starter (100% hydration)
- 1 1/2 cups (360ml) lukewarm water
- 3 cups (360g) spelt flour (whole grain or white)
- 1 teaspoon salt

Instructions:

Mix the Dough:
- In a large mixing bowl, combine the active sourdough starter and lukewarm water. Stir until the starter is dissolved in the water.
- Add the spelt flour and salt to the bowl. Mix until a shaggy dough forms and all the flour is hydrated.

Bulk Fermentation:
- Cover the bowl with a clean kitchen towel or plastic wrap and let the dough rest at room temperature for about 4-6 hours. During this time, perform a series of stretch and folds every 30 minutes for the first 2 hours to develop gluten.

Shape the Dough:
- After the bulk fermentation, lightly flour a work surface. Carefully transfer the dough onto the floured surface.
- Gently shape the dough into a round or oval loaf, being careful not to deflate it too much.

Final Proofing:
- Place the shaped loaf onto a piece of parchment paper. Cover the loaf with a clean kitchen towel and let it proof at room temperature for 1-2 hours, or until it has visibly increased in size and is puffy.

Preheat the Oven:
- About 30 minutes before the final proofing is complete, preheat your oven to 450°F (230°C). Place a Dutch oven or baking stone on the middle rack of the oven during preheating.

Score the Loaf:
- Once the oven is preheated and the dough has finished proofing, carefully score the top of the loaf with a sharp knife or bread lame to create decorative slashes.

Bake the Loaf:
- Carefully transfer the scored loaf, still on the parchment paper, into the preheated Dutch oven or onto the preheated baking stone.
- Bake the loaf covered for 20-25 minutes to create steam, then remove the lid or cover and continue baking for an additional 20-25 minutes, or until the crust is golden brown and the loaf sounds hollow when tapped on the bottom.

Cool and Enjoy:
- Once baked, transfer the loaf to a wire rack to cool completely before slicing. Enjoy your Sourdough Spelt Bread with your favorite toppings or spreads!

This Sourdough Spelt Bread offers a unique flavor and texture from the spelt flour, making it a delicious and wholesome addition to your bread repertoire. Enjoy its nutty flavor and hearty crumb!

Sourdough Kamut Bread

Ingredients:

- 1 cup (240g) active sourdough starter (100% hydration)
- 1 1/2 cups (360ml) lukewarm water
- 3 cups (360g) kamut flour
- 1 teaspoon salt

Instructions:

Mixing the Dough:
- In a large mixing bowl, combine the active sourdough starter and lukewarm water. Stir until the starter is dissolved in the water.
- Add the kamut flour and salt to the bowl. Mix until a shaggy dough forms and all the flour is hydrated.

Bulk Fermentation:
- Cover the bowl with a clean kitchen towel or plastic wrap and let the dough rest at room temperature for about 4-6 hours. During this time, perform a series of stretch and folds every 30 minutes for the first 2 hours to develop gluten.

Shaping the Dough:
- After the bulk fermentation, lightly flour a work surface. Carefully transfer the dough onto the floured surface.
- Gently shape the dough into a round or oval loaf, being careful not to deflate it too much.

Final Proofing:
- Place the shaped loaf onto a piece of parchment paper. Cover the loaf with a clean kitchen towel and let it proof at room temperature for 1-2 hours, or until it has visibly increased in size and is puffy.

Preheating the Oven:
- About 30 minutes before the final proofing is complete, preheat your oven to 450°F (230°C). Place a Dutch oven or baking stone on the middle rack of the oven during preheating.

Scoring the Loaf:
- Once the oven is preheated and the dough has finished proofing, carefully score the top of the loaf with a sharp knife or bread lame to create decorative slashes.

Baking the Loaf:

- Carefully transfer the scored loaf, still on the parchment paper, into the preheated Dutch oven or onto the preheated baking stone.
- Bake the loaf covered for 20-25 minutes to create steam, then remove the lid or cover and continue baking for an additional 20-25 minutes, or until the crust is golden brown and the loaf sounds hollow when tapped on the bottom.

Cooling and Enjoyment:
- Once baked, transfer the loaf to a wire rack to cool completely before slicing. Enjoy your Sourdough Kamut Bread with your favorite toppings or spreads!

This Sourdough Kamut Bread showcases the nutty flavor and tender texture of kamut flour, making it a delightful and wholesome addition to your bread repertoire. Enjoy its unique taste and nutritional benefits!

Sourdough Einkorn Bread

Ingredients:

- 1 cup (240g) active sourdough starter (100% hydration)
- 1 1/2 cups (360ml) lukewarm water
- 3 cups (360g) einkorn flour
- 1 teaspoon salt

Instructions:

Mixing the Dough:
- In a large mixing bowl, combine the active sourdough starter and lukewarm water. Stir until the starter is dissolved in the water.
- Add the einkorn flour and salt to the bowl. Mix until a shaggy dough forms and all the flour is hydrated.

Bulk Fermentation:
- Cover the bowl with a clean kitchen towel or plastic wrap and let the dough rest at room temperature for about 4-6 hours. During this time, perform a series of stretch and folds every 30 minutes for the first 2 hours to develop gluten.

Shaping the Dough:
- After the bulk fermentation, lightly flour a work surface. Carefully transfer the dough onto the floured surface.
- Gently shape the dough into a round or oval loaf, being careful not to deflate it too much.

Final Proofing:
- Place the shaped loaf onto a piece of parchment paper. Cover the loaf with a clean kitchen towel and let it proof at room temperature for 1-2 hours, or until it has visibly increased in size and is puffy.

Preheating the Oven:
- About 30 minutes before the final proofing is complete, preheat your oven to 450°F (230°C). Place a Dutch oven or baking stone on the middle rack of the oven during preheating.

Scoring the Loaf:
- Once the oven is preheated and the dough has finished proofing, carefully score the top of the loaf with a sharp knife or bread lame to create decorative slashes.

Baking the Loaf:
- Carefully transfer the scored loaf, still on the parchment paper, into the preheated Dutch oven or onto the preheated baking stone.
- Bake the loaf covered for 20-25 minutes to create steam, then remove the lid or cover and continue baking for an additional 20-25 minutes, or until the crust is golden brown and the loaf sounds hollow when tapped on the bottom.

Cooling and Enjoyment:
- Once baked, transfer the loaf to a wire rack to cool completely before slicing. Enjoy your Sourdough Einkorn Bread with your favorite toppings or spreads!

This Sourdough Einkorn Bread showcases the unique flavor and texture of einkorn flour, making it a delightful and nutritious addition to your bread repertoire. Enjoy its distinct taste and wholesome qualities!

Sourdough Emmer Bread

Ingredients:

- 1 cup (240g) active sourdough starter (100% hydration)
- 1 1/2 cups (360ml) lukewarm water
- 3 cups (360g) whole grain emmer flour
- 1 teaspoon salt

Instructions:

Mixing the Dough:
- In a large mixing bowl, combine the active sourdough starter and lukewarm water. Stir until the starter is dissolved in the water.
- Add the whole grain emmer flour and salt to the bowl. Mix until a shaggy dough forms and all the flour is hydrated.

Bulk Fermentation:
- Cover the bowl with a clean kitchen towel or plastic wrap and let the dough rest at room temperature for about 4-6 hours. During this time, perform a series of stretch and folds every 30 minutes for the first 2 hours to develop gluten.

Shaping the Dough:
- After the bulk fermentation, lightly flour a work surface. Carefully transfer the dough onto the floured surface.
- Gently shape the dough into a round or oval loaf, being careful not to deflate it too much.

Final Proofing:
- Place the shaped loaf onto a piece of parchment paper. Cover the loaf with a clean kitchen towel and let it proof at room temperature for 1-2 hours, or until it has visibly increased in size and is puffy.

Preheating the Oven:
- About 30 minutes before the final proofing is complete, preheat your oven to 450°F (230°C). Place a Dutch oven or baking stone on the middle rack of the oven during preheating.

Scoring the Loaf:
- Once the oven is preheated and the dough has finished proofing, carefully score the top of the loaf with a sharp knife or bread lame to create decorative slashes.

Baking the Loaf:
- Carefully transfer the scored loaf, still on the parchment paper, into the preheated Dutch oven or onto the preheated baking stone.
- Bake the loaf covered for 20-25 minutes to create steam, then remove the lid or cover and continue baking for an additional 20-25 minutes, or until the crust is golden brown and the loaf sounds hollow when tapped on the bottom.

Cooling and Enjoyment:
- Once baked, transfer the loaf to a wire rack to cool completely before slicing. Enjoy your Sourdough Emmer Bread with your favorite toppings or spreads!

This Sourdough Emmer Bread showcases the nutty flavor and rustic texture of emmer flour, making it a delicious and wholesome addition to your bread repertoire. Enjoy its unique taste and nutritional benefits!

Sourdough Feta and Spinach Bread

Ingredients:

- 1 cup (240g) active sourdough starter (100% hydration)
- 1 1/2 cups (360ml) lukewarm water
- 4 cups (500g) bread flour
- 1 teaspoon salt
- 1 cup (150g) crumbled feta cheese
- 1 cup (100g) chopped fresh spinach leaves

Instructions:

Mixing the Dough:
- In a large mixing bowl, combine the active sourdough starter and lukewarm water. Stir until the starter is dissolved in the water.
- Add the bread flour and salt to the bowl. Mix until a shaggy dough forms and all the flour is hydrated.
- Fold in the crumbled feta cheese and chopped fresh spinach leaves until evenly distributed throughout the dough.

Bulk Fermentation:
- Cover the bowl with a clean kitchen towel or plastic wrap and let the dough rest at room temperature for about 4-6 hours. During this time, perform a series of stretch and folds every 30 minutes for the first 2 hours to develop gluten.

Shaping the Dough:
- After the bulk fermentation, lightly flour a work surface. Carefully transfer the dough onto the floured surface.
- Gently shape the dough into a round or oval loaf, being careful not to deflate it too much.

Final Proofing:
- Place the shaped loaf onto a piece of parchment paper. Cover the loaf with a clean kitchen towel and let it proof at room temperature for 1-2 hours, or until it has visibly increased in size and is puffy.

Preheating the Oven:
- About 30 minutes before the final proofing is complete, preheat your oven to 450°F (230°C). Place a Dutch oven or baking stone on the middle rack of the oven during preheating.

Scoring the Loaf:
- Once the oven is preheated and the dough has finished proofing, carefully score the top of the loaf with a sharp knife or bread lame to create decorative slashes.

Baking the Loaf:
- Carefully transfer the scored loaf, still on the parchment paper, into the preheated Dutch oven or onto the preheated baking stone.
- Bake the loaf covered for 20-25 minutes to create steam, then remove the lid or cover and continue baking for an additional 20-25 minutes, or until the crust is golden brown and the loaf sounds hollow when tapped on the bottom.

Cooling and Enjoyment:
- Once baked, transfer the loaf to a wire rack to cool completely before slicing. Enjoy your Sourdough Feta and Spinach Bread with your favorite toppings or spreads!

This Sourdough Feta and Spinach Bread is packed with flavor from the tangy feta cheese and fresh spinach, making it a delicious and savory option for sandwiches, toast, or enjoyed on its own. Enjoy its unique taste and wholesome ingredients!

Sourdough Sun-Dried Tomato Bread

Ingredients:

- 1 cup (240g) active sourdough starter (100% hydration)
- 1 1/2 cups (360ml) lukewarm water
- 4 cups (500g) bread flour
- 1 teaspoon salt
- 1/2 cup (75g) chopped sun-dried tomatoes (drained if packed in oil)
- 2 tablespoons (30ml) oil from the jar of sun-dried tomatoes (optional, for extra flavor)

Instructions:

Mixing the Dough:
- In a large mixing bowl, combine the active sourdough starter and lukewarm water. Stir until the starter is dissolved in the water.
- Add the bread flour and salt to the bowl. Mix until a shaggy dough forms and all the flour is hydrated.
- Fold in the chopped sun-dried tomatoes and oil from the jar, if using, until evenly distributed throughout the dough.

Bulk Fermentation:
- Cover the bowl with a clean kitchen towel or plastic wrap and let the dough rest at room temperature for about 4-6 hours. During this time, perform a series of stretch and folds every 30 minutes for the first 2 hours to develop gluten.

Shaping the Dough:
- After the bulk fermentation, lightly flour a work surface. Carefully transfer the dough onto the floured surface.
- Gently shape the dough into a round or oval loaf, being careful not to deflate it too much.

Final Proofing:
- Place the shaped loaf onto a piece of parchment paper. Cover the loaf with a clean kitchen towel and let it proof at room temperature for 1-2 hours, or until it has visibly increased in size and is puffy.

Preheating the Oven:

- About 30 minutes before the final proofing is complete, preheat your oven to 450°F (230°C). Place a Dutch oven or baking stone on the middle rack of the oven during preheating.

Scoring the Loaf:
- Once the oven is preheated and the dough has finished proofing, carefully score the top of the loaf with a sharp knife or bread lame to create decorative slashes.

Baking the Loaf:
- Carefully transfer the scored loaf, still on the parchment paper, into the preheated Dutch oven or onto the preheated baking stone.
- Bake the loaf covered for 20-25 minutes to create steam, then remove the lid or cover and continue baking for an additional 20-25 minutes, or until the crust is golden brown and the loaf sounds hollow when tapped on the bottom.

Cooling and Enjoyment:
- Once baked, transfer the loaf to a wire rack to cool completely before slicing. Enjoy your Sourdough Sun-Dried Tomato Bread with your favorite toppings or spreads!

This Sourdough Sun-Dried Tomato Bread is packed with flavor from the sweet and tangy sun-dried tomatoes, making it a delicious and savory option for sandwiches, toast, or enjoyed on its own. Enjoy its unique taste and wholesome ingredients!

Sourdough Asiago and Rosemary Bread

Ingredients:

- 1 cup (240g) active sourdough starter (100% hydration)
- 1 1/2 cups (360ml) lukewarm water
- 4 cups (500g) bread flour
- 1 teaspoon salt
- 1 cup (100g) shredded Asiago cheese
- 2 tablespoons fresh rosemary, finely chopped

Instructions:

Mixing the Dough:
- In a large mixing bowl, combine the active sourdough starter and lukewarm water. Stir until the starter is dissolved in the water.
- Add the bread flour and salt to the bowl. Mix until a shaggy dough forms and all the flour is hydrated.
- Fold in the shredded Asiago cheese and chopped fresh rosemary until evenly distributed throughout the dough.

Bulk Fermentation:
- Cover the bowl with a clean kitchen towel or plastic wrap and let the dough rest at room temperature for about 4-6 hours. During this time, perform a series of stretch and folds every 30 minutes for the first 2 hours to develop gluten.

Shaping the Dough:
- After the bulk fermentation, lightly flour a work surface. Carefully transfer the dough onto the floured surface.
- Gently shape the dough into a round or oval loaf, being careful not to deflate it too much.

Final Proofing:
- Place the shaped loaf onto a piece of parchment paper. Cover the loaf with a clean kitchen towel and let it proof at room temperature for 1-2 hours, or until it has visibly increased in size and is puffy.

Preheating the Oven:
- About 30 minutes before the final proofing is complete, preheat your oven to 450°F (230°C). Place a Dutch oven or baking stone on the middle rack of the oven during preheating.

Scoring the Loaf:
- Once the oven is preheated and the dough has finished proofing, carefully score the top of the loaf with a sharp knife or bread lame to create decorative slashes.

Baking the Loaf:
- Carefully transfer the scored loaf, still on the parchment paper, into the preheated Dutch oven or onto the preheated baking stone.
- Bake the loaf covered for 20-25 minutes to create steam, then remove the lid or cover and continue baking for an additional 20-25 minutes, or until the crust is golden brown and the loaf sounds hollow when tapped on the bottom.

Cooling and Enjoyment:
- Once baked, transfer the loaf to a wire rack to cool completely before slicing. Enjoy your Sourdough Asiago and Rosemary Bread with your favorite toppings or spreads!

This Sourdough Asiago and Rosemary Bread is bursting with flavor from the savory Asiago cheese and aromatic rosemary, making it a delicious and aromatic option for sandwiches, toast, or enjoyed on its own. Enjoy its rich taste and wholesome ingredients!

Sourdough Pesto Swirl Bread

Ingredients:

- 1 cup (240g) active sourdough starter (100% hydration)
- 1 1/2 cups (360ml) lukewarm water
- 4 cups (500g) bread flour
- 1 teaspoon salt
- 1 cup (100g) shredded Asiago cheese
- 2 tablespoons fresh rosemary, finely chopped

Instructions:

Mixing the Dough:
- In a large mixing bowl, combine the active sourdough starter and lukewarm water. Stir until the starter is dissolved in the water.
- Add the bread flour and salt to the bowl. Mix until a shaggy dough forms and all the flour is hydrated.
- Fold in the shredded Asiago cheese and chopped fresh rosemary until evenly distributed throughout the dough.

Bulk Fermentation:
- Cover the bowl with a clean kitchen towel or plastic wrap and let the dough rest at room temperature for about 4-6 hours. During this time, perform a series of stretch and folds every 30 minutes for the first 2 hours to develop gluten.

Shaping the Dough:
- After the bulk fermentation, lightly flour a work surface. Carefully transfer the dough onto the floured surface.
- Gently shape the dough into a round or oval loaf, being careful not to deflate it too much.

Final Proofing:
- Place the shaped loaf onto a piece of parchment paper. Cover the loaf with a clean kitchen towel and let it proof at room temperature for 1-2 hours, or until it has visibly increased in size and is puffy.

Preheating the Oven:
- About 30 minutes before the final proofing is complete, preheat your oven to 450°F (230°C). Place a Dutch oven or baking stone on the middle rack of the oven during preheating.

Scoring the Loaf:
- Once the oven is preheated and the dough has finished proofing, carefully score the top of the loaf with a sharp knife or bread lame to create decorative slashes.

Baking the Loaf:
- Carefully transfer the scored loaf, still on the parchment paper, into the preheated Dutch oven or onto the preheated baking stone.
- Bake the loaf covered for 20-25 minutes to create steam, then remove the lid or cover and continue baking for an additional 20-25 minutes, or until the crust is golden brown and the loaf sounds hollow when tapped on the bottom.

Cooling and Enjoyment:
- Once baked, transfer the loaf to a wire rack to cool completely before slicing. Enjoy your Sourdough Asiago and Rosemary Bread with your favorite toppings or spreads!

This Sourdough Asiago and Rosemary Bread is bursting with flavor from the savory Asiago cheese and aromatic rosemary, making it a delicious and aromatic option for sandwiches, toast, or enjoyed on its own. Enjoy its rich taste and wholesome ingredients!

Sourdough Pesto Swirl Bread

Ingredients:

For the dough:

- 1 cup (240g) active sourdough starter (100% hydration)
- 1 1/2 cups (360ml) lukewarm water
- 4 cups (500g) bread flour
- 1 teaspoon salt

For the pesto filling:

- 1 cup fresh basil leaves
- 1/4 cup (60ml) olive oil
- 1/4 cup (25g) grated Parmesan cheese
- 2 cloves garlic, minced
- Salt and pepper to taste

Instructions:

Make the Pesto:
- In a food processor, combine the fresh basil leaves, olive oil, grated Parmesan cheese, minced garlic, salt, and pepper. Blend until smooth. Set aside.

Mixing the Dough:
- In a large mixing bowl, combine the active sourdough starter and lukewarm water. Stir until the starter is dissolved in the water.
- Add the bread flour and salt to the bowl. Mix until a shaggy dough forms and all the flour is hydrated.

Bulk Fermentation:
- Cover the bowl with a clean kitchen towel or plastic wrap and let the dough rest at room temperature for about 4-6 hours. During this time, perform a series of stretch and folds every 30 minutes for the first 2 hours to develop gluten.

Shaping the Dough:

- After the bulk fermentation, lightly flour a work surface. Carefully transfer the dough onto the floured surface.
- Gently shape the dough into a rectangle, about 12x18 inches in size.

Spread the Pesto:
- Evenly spread the pesto mixture over the surface of the dough rectangle, leaving a small border around the edges.

Roll the Dough:
- Starting from one of the long sides, tightly roll the dough into a log shape, similar to rolling cinnamon rolls.

Final Proofing:
- Place the rolled dough into a greased loaf pan, seam side down. Cover the loaf pan with a clean kitchen towel and let it proof at room temperature for 1-2 hours, or until it has visibly increased in size and is puffy.

Preheating the Oven:
- About 30 minutes before the final proofing is complete, preheat your oven to 450°F (230°C).

Baking the Loaf:
- Once the dough has finished proofing, bake it in the preheated oven for 35-40 minutes, or until the crust is golden brown and the loaf sounds hollow when tapped on the bottom.

Cooling and Enjoyment:
- Once baked, remove the loaf from the oven and let it cool in the pan for 10 minutes before transferring it to a wire rack to cool completely. Slice and enjoy your delicious Sourdough Pesto Swirl Bread!

This Sourdough Pesto Swirl Bread is packed with the vibrant flavors of fresh basil, garlic, and Parmesan cheese, making it a delightful and savory option for sandwiches, toast, or enjoyed on its own. Enjoy its rich taste and beautiful swirls!

Sourdough Olive Oil Bread

Ingredients:

- 1 cup (240g) active sourdough starter (100% hydration)
- 1 1/2 cups (360ml) lukewarm water
- 2 tablespoons (30ml) olive oil
- 4 cups (500g) bread flour
- 1 teaspoon salt

Instructions:

Mixing the Dough:
- In a large mixing bowl, combine the active sourdough starter, lukewarm water, and olive oil. Stir until well combined.
- Add the bread flour and salt to the bowl. Mix until a shaggy dough forms and all the flour is hydrated.

Kneading and Stretching:
- Turn the dough out onto a lightly floured surface. Knead the dough for about 10-15 minutes until it becomes smooth and elastic. You can also perform a series of stretch and folds every 30 minutes for the first 2 hours to develop gluten.

Bulk Fermentation:
- Place the kneaded dough back into the mixing bowl. Cover the bowl with a clean kitchen towel or plastic wrap and let the dough rest at room temperature for about 4-6 hours, or until it has doubled in size.

Shaping the Dough:
- After the bulk fermentation, gently deflate the dough and shape it into a round or oval loaf.

Final Proofing:
- Place the shaped loaf onto a piece of parchment paper. Cover the loaf with a clean kitchen towel and let it proof at room temperature for 1-2 hours, or until it has visibly increased in size and is puffy.

Preheating the Oven:
- About 30 minutes before the final proofing is complete, preheat your oven to 450°F (230°C). Place a Dutch oven or baking stone on the middle rack of the oven during preheating.

Scoring the Loaf:

- Once the oven is preheated and the dough has finished proofing, carefully score the top of the loaf with a sharp knife or bread lame to create decorative slashes.

Baking the Loaf:
- Carefully transfer the scored loaf, still on the parchment paper, into the preheated Dutch oven or onto the preheated baking stone.
- Bake the loaf covered for 20-25 minutes to create steam, then remove the lid or cover and continue baking for an additional 20-25 minutes, or until the crust is golden brown and the loaf sounds hollow when tapped on the bottom.

Cooling and Enjoyment:
- Once baked, transfer the loaf to a wire rack to cool completely before slicing. Enjoy your Sourdough Olive Oil Bread with your favorite toppings or spreads!

This Sourdough Olive Oil Bread is enriched with the subtle flavor of olive oil and has a tender crumb, making it perfect for sandwiches, toast, or served alongside soups and salads. Enjoy its simplicity and delicious taste!

Sourdough Honey Wheat Bread

Ingredients:

- 1 cup (240g) active sourdough starter (100% hydration)
- 1 1/2 cups (360ml) lukewarm water
- 2 tablespoons (30ml) honey
- 2 tablespoons (30ml) olive oil or melted butter
- 3 cups (375g) whole wheat flour
- 1 cup (125g) bread flour (plus extra for dusting)
- 1 1/2 teaspoons salt

Instructions:

Mixing the Dough:
- In a large mixing bowl, combine the active sourdough starter, lukewarm water, honey, and olive oil (or melted butter). Stir until well combined.
- Add the whole wheat flour, bread flour, and salt to the bowl. Mix until a shaggy dough forms and all the flour is hydrated.

Kneading and Stretching:
- Turn the dough out onto a lightly floured surface. Knead the dough for about 10-15 minutes until it becomes smooth and elastic. You can also perform a series of stretch and folds every 30 minutes for the first 2 hours to develop gluten.

Bulk Fermentation:
- Place the kneaded dough back into the mixing bowl. Cover the bowl with a clean kitchen towel or plastic wrap and let the dough rest at room temperature for about 4-6 hours, or until it has doubled in size.

Shaping the Dough:
- After the bulk fermentation, gently deflate the dough and shape it into a round or oval loaf.

Final Proofing:
- Place the shaped loaf onto a piece of parchment paper. Cover the loaf with a clean kitchen towel and let it proof at room temperature for 1-2 hours, or until it has visibly increased in size and is puffy.

Preheating the Oven:

- About 30 minutes before the final proofing is complete, preheat your oven to 450°F (230°C). Place a Dutch oven or baking stone on the middle rack of the oven during preheating.

Scoring the Loaf:
- Once the oven is preheated and the dough has finished proofing, carefully score the top of the loaf with a sharp knife or bread lame to create decorative slashes.

Baking the Loaf:
- Carefully transfer the scored loaf, still on the parchment paper, into the preheated Dutch oven or onto the preheated baking stone.
- Bake the loaf covered for 20-25 minutes to create steam, then remove the lid or cover and continue baking for an additional 20-25 minutes, or until the crust is golden brown and the loaf sounds hollow when tapped on the bottom.

Cooling and Enjoyment:
- Once baked, transfer the loaf to a wire rack to cool completely before slicing. Enjoy your Sourdough Honey Wheat Bread with your favorite toppings or spreads!

This Sourdough Honey Wheat Bread is lightly sweetened with honey and has a hearty whole wheat flavor, making it perfect for sandwiches, toast, or enjoyed on its own. Enjoy its wholesome taste and nourishing ingredients!

Sourdough Irish Soda Bread

Ingredients:

- 1 cup (240g) active sourdough starter (100% hydration)
- 1 1/2 cups (360ml) buttermilk
- 4 cups (500g) all-purpose flour
- 1 teaspoon salt
- 1 teaspoon baking soda

Instructions:

Preheat the Oven: Preheat your oven to 425°F (220°C). Lightly grease a baking sheet or line it with parchment paper.

Mix the Ingredients: In a large mixing bowl, combine the active sourdough starter and buttermilk. Stir until well combined.

Add Dry Ingredients: Add the all-purpose flour, salt, and baking soda to the bowl. Mix until a shaggy dough forms and all the flour is hydrated. If the dough is too dry, you can add a little more buttermilk.

Shape the Dough: Turn the dough out onto a lightly floured surface. Shape it into a round loaf, about 8 inches (20cm) in diameter. Place the loaf onto the prepared baking sheet.

Score the Dough: Use a sharp knife to score a deep cross into the top of the loaf. This helps the bread to bake evenly and creates the traditional look of Irish soda bread.

Bake the Bread: Transfer the baking sheet to the preheated oven and bake for 35-40 minutes, or until the bread is golden brown and sounds hollow when tapped on the bottom.

Cool and Serve: Once baked, transfer the bread to a wire rack to cool completely before slicing. Serve with butter, jam, or your favorite toppings.

This Sourdough Irish Soda Bread has a wonderful tangy flavor from the sourdough starter and buttermilk, and it's perfect for serving alongside soups, stews, or as part of a St. Patrick's Day celebration. Enjoy its rustic texture and delicious taste!

Sourdough Caramelized Onion Bread

Ingredients:

- 1 cup (240g) active sourdough starter (100% hydration)
- 1 1/2 cups (360ml) lukewarm water
- 4 cups (500g) bread flour
- 1 teaspoon salt
- 2 tablespoons (30ml) olive oil
- 1 large onion, thinly sliced
- 1 tablespoon (15g) butter
- 1 teaspoon sugar
- Salt and pepper to taste

Instructions:

Prepare the Caramelized Onions:
- In a skillet, melt the butter over medium heat. Add the thinly sliced onion and cook, stirring occasionally, until the onions are soft and golden brown, about 20-25 minutes.
- Sprinkle the sugar over the onions and continue cooking for another 5 minutes, stirring occasionally, until the onions are caramelized. Season with salt and pepper to taste. Remove from heat and let cool.

Mixing the Dough:
- In a large mixing bowl, combine the active sourdough starter and lukewarm water. Stir until the starter is dissolved in the water.
- Add the bread flour, salt, and olive oil to the bowl. Mix until a shaggy dough forms and all the flour is hydrated.
- Fold in the caramelized onions until evenly distributed throughout the dough.

Bulk Fermentation:
- Cover the bowl with a clean kitchen towel or plastic wrap and let the dough rest at room temperature for about 4-6 hours, or until it has doubled in size. During this time, perform a series of stretch and folds every 30 minutes for the first 2 hours to develop gluten.

Shaping the Dough:
- After the bulk fermentation, lightly flour a work surface. Carefully transfer the dough onto the floured surface.

- Gently shape the dough into a round or oval loaf, being careful not to deflate it too much.

Final Proofing:
- Place the shaped loaf onto a piece of parchment paper. Cover the loaf with a clean kitchen towel and let it proof at room temperature for 1-2 hours, or until it has visibly increased in size and is puffy.

Preheating the Oven:
- About 30 minutes before the final proofing is complete, preheat your oven to 450°F (230°C). Place a Dutch oven or baking stone on the middle rack of the oven during preheating.

Scoring the Loaf:
- Once the oven is preheated and the dough has finished proofing, carefully score the top of the loaf with a sharp knife or bread lame to create decorative slashes.

Baking the Loaf:
- Carefully transfer the scored loaf, still on the parchment paper, into the preheated Dutch oven or onto the preheated baking stone.
- Bake the loaf covered for 20-25 minutes to create steam, then remove the lid or cover and continue baking for an additional 20-25 minutes, or until the crust is golden brown and the loaf sounds hollow when tapped on the bottom.

Cooling and Enjoyment:
- Once baked, transfer the loaf to a wire rack to cool completely before slicing. Enjoy your Sourdough Caramelized Onion Bread with your favorite toppings or spreads!

This Sourdough Caramelized Onion Bread is filled with the rich flavor of caramelized onions, making it a delicious and savory option for sandwiches, toast, or enjoyed on its own. Enjoy its unique taste and wholesome ingredients!

Sourdough Garlic Bread

Ingredients:

- 1 loaf of sourdough bread (French or Italian loaf)
- 1/2 cup (115g) unsalted butter, softened
- 4 cloves garlic, minced
- 2 tablespoons fresh parsley, finely chopped
- Salt and pepper to taste

Instructions:

Preheat the Oven: Preheat your oven to 375°F (190°C).

Prepare the Garlic Butter:
- In a small mixing bowl, combine the softened butter, minced garlic, chopped parsley, salt, and pepper. Mix until well combined.

Prepare the Bread:
- Using a serrated knife, slice the sourdough bread loaf horizontally, but not all the way through, leaving the bottom crust intact.

Spread the Garlic Butter:
- Open up the sliced bread and generously spread the garlic butter mixture between the slices, making sure to cover both sides of each slice.

Wrap the Bread:
- Wrap the prepared loaf in aluminum foil, leaving the top exposed.

Bake the Bread:
- Place the wrapped loaf on a baking sheet and transfer it to the preheated oven. Bake for 15-20 minutes, or until the bread is heated through and the garlic butter is melted and fragrant.

Optional Broiling:
- If desired, unwrap the top of the loaf and broil for an additional 2-3 minutes, or until the top is golden brown and crispy.

Serve:
- Remove the garlic bread from the oven and let it cool for a few minutes before slicing. Serve warm and enjoy!

This Sourdough Garlic Bread is perfect as a side dish for pasta, soups, salads, or served as an appetizer. It's loaded with garlic and buttery flavor, making it a delicious addition to any meal. Enjoy its crispy exterior and soft, flavorful interior!

Sourdough Herb and Cheese Bread

Ingredients:

- 1 cup (240g) active sourdough starter (100% hydration)
- 1 1/2 cups (360ml) lukewarm water
- 4 cups (500g) bread flour
- 1 teaspoon salt
- 1/2 cup (60g) grated cheese (such as cheddar, Parmesan, or Gruyere)
- 2 tablespoons mixed dried herbs (such as thyme, rosemary, oregano, and basil)
- Additional grated cheese and herbs for topping (optional)

Instructions:

Mixing the Dough:
- In a large mixing bowl, combine the active sourdough starter and lukewarm water. Stir until the starter is dissolved in the water.
- Add the bread flour and salt to the bowl. Mix until a shaggy dough forms and all the flour is hydrated.
- Fold in the grated cheese and mixed dried herbs until evenly distributed throughout the dough.

Bulk Fermentation:
- Cover the bowl with a clean kitchen towel or plastic wrap and let the dough rest at room temperature for about 4-6 hours. During this time, perform a series of stretch and folds every 30 minutes for the first 2 hours to develop gluten.

Shaping the Dough:
- After the bulk fermentation, lightly flour a work surface. Carefully transfer the dough onto the floured surface.
- Gently shape the dough into a round or oval loaf, being careful not to deflate it too much.

Final Proofing:
- Place the shaped loaf onto a piece of parchment paper. Cover the loaf with a clean kitchen towel and let it proof at room temperature for 1-2 hours, or until it has visibly increased in size and is puffy.

Preheating the Oven:

- About 30 minutes before the final proofing is complete, preheat your oven to 450°F (230°C). Place a Dutch oven or baking stone on the middle rack of the oven during preheating.

Scoring the Loaf:
- Once the oven is preheated and the dough has finished proofing, carefully score the top of the loaf with a sharp knife or bread lame to create decorative slashes.

Baking the Loaf:
- Carefully transfer the scored loaf, still on the parchment paper, into the preheated Dutch oven or onto the preheated baking stone.
- Optionally, sprinkle additional grated cheese and herbs on top of the loaf.
- Bake the loaf covered for 20-25 minutes to create steam, then remove the lid or cover and continue baking for an additional 20-25 minutes, or until the crust is golden brown and the loaf sounds hollow when tapped on the bottom.

Cooling and Enjoyment:
- Once baked, transfer the loaf to a wire rack to cool completely before slicing. Enjoy your Sourdough Herb and Cheese Bread with your favorite toppings or spreads!

This Sourdough Herb and Cheese Bread is bursting with flavor from the savory cheese and aromatic herbs, making it a delicious and aromatic option for sandwiches, toast, or enjoyed on its own. Enjoy its rich taste and wholesome ingredients!

Sourdough Everything Bagel Bread

Ingredients:

For the dough:

- 1 cup (240g) active sourdough starter (100% hydration)
- 1 1/2 cups (360ml) lukewarm water
- 4 cups (500g) bread flour
- 1 teaspoon salt

For the everything bagel seasoning:

- 2 tablespoons sesame seeds
- 2 tablespoons poppy seeds
- 1 tablespoon dried minced garlic
- 1 tablespoon dried minced onion
- 1 tablespoon coarse salt

Instructions:

Mixing the Dough:
- In a large mixing bowl, combine the active sourdough starter and lukewarm water. Stir until the starter is dissolved in the water.
- Add the bread flour and salt to the bowl. Mix until a shaggy dough forms and all the flour is hydrated.

Bulk Fermentation:
- Cover the bowl with a clean kitchen towel or plastic wrap and let the dough rest at room temperature for about 4-6 hours. During this time, perform a series of stretch and folds every 30 minutes for the first 2 hours to develop gluten.

Shaping the Dough:
- After the bulk fermentation, lightly flour a work surface. Carefully transfer the dough onto the floured surface.
- Gently shape the dough into a round or oval loaf, being careful not to deflate it too much.

Final Proofing:

- Place the shaped loaf onto a piece of parchment paper. Cover the loaf with a clean kitchen towel and let it proof at room temperature for 1-2 hours, or until it has visibly increased in size and is puffy.

Preheating the Oven:
- About 30 minutes before the final proofing is complete, preheat your oven to 450°F (230°C). Place a Dutch oven or baking stone on the middle rack of the oven during preheating.

Preparing the Everything Bagel Seasoning:
- In a small bowl, combine the sesame seeds, poppy seeds, dried minced garlic, dried minced onion, and coarse salt. Mix until well combined.

Scoring the Loaf and Adding Seasoning:
- Once the oven is preheated and the dough has finished proofing, carefully score the top of the loaf with a sharp knife or bread lame.
- Generously sprinkle the everything bagel seasoning mixture over the top of the loaf, pressing lightly to adhere.

Baking the Loaf:
- Carefully transfer the scored and seasoned loaf, still on the parchment paper, into the preheated Dutch oven or onto the preheated baking stone.
- Bake the loaf covered for 20-25 minutes to create steam, then remove the lid or cover and continue baking for an additional 20-25 minutes, or until the crust is golden brown and the loaf sounds hollow when tapped on the bottom.

Cooling and Enjoyment:
- Once baked, transfer the loaf to a wire rack to cool completely before slicing. Enjoy your Sourdough Everything Bagel Bread with your favorite spreads or toppings!

This Sourdough Everything Bagel Bread is packed with the classic flavors of sesame seeds, poppy seeds, garlic, onion, and salt, making it a delicious and flavorful option for sandwiches, toast, or enjoyed on its own. Enjoy its rich taste and wholesome ingredients!

www.ingramcontent.com/pod-product-compliance
Lightning Source LLC
LaVergne TN
LVHW081558060526
838201LV00054B/1961